Lektürehilfen
Aldous Huxley
»Brave New World«

Barron's Book Notes
Ernst Klett Verlag
Stuttgart Düsseldorf Leipzig

Reihe: Lektürehilfen Englisch
Verfasser dieses Bandes: Anthony Astrachan

Gedruckt auf Recyclingpapier, das aus
100 % Altpapier hergestellt wurde.

Die Deutsche Bibliothek – CIP-Einheitsaufnahme

Astrachan, Anthony:
Lektürehilfen Aldous Huxley, „Brave new world" /
[Verf. dieses Bd.: Anthony Astrachan]. – 10. Aufl. –
Stuttgart ; Düsseldorf ; Leipzig : Klett, 1998
ISBN 3-12-922224-3

10. Auflage 1998

Abbildung auf der Titelseite: dpa
Druck: Wilhelm Röck, Weinsberg. Printed in Germany.
Einbandgestaltung: Bayerl & Ost, Frankfurt/M.
ISBN-3-12-922224-3

CONTENTS

HOW TO USE THIS BOOK

You have to know how to approach literature in order to get the most out of it. This *Barron's Book Notes* volume follows a plan based on methods used by some of the best students to read a work of literature.

Begin with the guide's section on the author's life and times. As you read, try to form a clear picture of the author's personality, circumstances, and motives for writing the work. This background usually will make it easier for you to hear the author's tone of voice, and follow where the author is heading.

Then go over the rest of the introductory material—such sections as those on the plot, characters, setting, themes, and style of the work. Underline, or write down in your notebook, particular things to watch for, such as contrasts between characters and repeated literary devices. At this point, you may want to develop a system of symbols to use in marking your text as you read. (Of course, you should only mark up a book you own, not one that belongs to another person or a school.) Perhaps you will want to use a different letter for each character's name, a different number for each major theme of the book, a different color for each important symbol or literary device. Be prepared to mark up the pages of your book as you read. Put your marks in the margins so you can find them again easily.

Now comes the moment you've been waiting for—the time to start reading the work of literature. You may want to put aside your *Barron's Book Notes* volume until you've read the work all the way through. Or you may want to alternate, reading the *Book Notes* analysis of each section as soon as you have finished reading the corresponding part of the original. Before you move on, reread crucial passages you don't fully understand. (Don't take this guide's analysis for granted—make up your own mind as to what the work means.)

Once you've finished the whole work of literature, you may want to review it right away, so you can firm up your ideas about what it means. You may want to leaf through the book concentrating on passages you marked in reference to one character or one theme. This is also a good time to reread the *Book Notes* introductory material, which pulls together insights on specific topics.

When it comes time to prepare for a test or to write a paper, you'll already have formed ideas about the work. You'll be able to go back through it, refreshing your memory as to the author's exact words and perspective, so that you can support your opinions with evidence drawn straight from the work. Patterns will emerge, and ideas will fall into place; your essay question or term paper will almost write itself. Give yourself a dry run with one of the sample tests in the guide. These tests present both multiple-choice and essay questions. An accompanying section gives answers to the multiple-choice questions as well as suggestions for writing the essays. If you have to select a term paper topic, you may choose one from the list of suggestions in this book. This guide also provides you with a reading list, to help you when you start research for a term paper, and a selection of provocative comments by critics, to spark your thinking before you write.

THE AUTHOR AND HIS TIMES

Aldous Leonard Huxley was born on July 26, 1894, into a family that included some of the most distinguished members of that part of the English ruling class made up of the intellectual elite. Aldous' father was the son of Thomas Henry Huxley, a great biologist who helped develop the theory of evolution. His mother was the sister of Mrs. Humphrey Ward, the novelist; the niece of Matthew Arnold, the poet; and the granddaughter of Thomas Arnold, a famous educator and the real-life headmaster of Rugby School who became a character in the novel *Tom Brown's Schooldays*.

Undoubtedly, Huxley's heritage and upbringing had an effect on his work. Gerald Heard, a longtime friend, said that Huxley's ancestry "brought down on him a weight of intellectual authority and a momentum of moral obligations." Throughout *Brave New World* you can see evidence of an ambivalent attitude toward such authority assumed by a ruling class.

Like the England of his day, Huxley's Utopia possesses a rigid class structure, one even stronger than England's because it is biologically and chemically engineered and psychologically conditioned. And the members of *Brave New World*'s ruling class certainly believe they possess the right to make everyone happy by denying them love and freedom.

Huxley's own experiences made him stand apart from the class into which he was born. Even as a small child he was considered different, showing an alertness, an intelligence, what his brother called a superiority. He was respected and loved—not hated—for these abilities, but he drew on that feeling of separateness in writing *Brave New World*. Bernard Marx and Helmholtz Watson, both members of the elite class, have problems because they're different from their peers. Huxley felt that heredity made each individual unique, and the uniqueness of the individual was essential to freedom. Like his family, and like the Alphas of *Brave New World*, Huxley felt a moral obligation—but it was the obligation to fight the idea that happiness could be achieved through class-instituted slavery of even the most benevolent kind.

Another event that marked Huxley was his mother's death from cancer when he was 14. This, he said later, gave him a sense of the transience of human happiness. Perhaps you can also see the influence of his loss in *Brave New World*. The Utopians go to great lengths to deny the unpleasantness of death, and to find perpetual happiness. But the cost is very great. By denying themselves unpleasant emotions they deny themselves deeply joyous ones as well. Their happiness can be continued endlessly by taking the drug *soma*, by making love, or by playing Obstacle Golf, but this happiness is essentially shallow. Standing in contrast to the Utopians are the Savages on the Reservation in New Mexico: poor, dirty, subject to the ills of old age and painful death, but, Huxley seems to believe, blessed with a happiness that while still transient is deeper and more real than that enjoyed by the inhabitants of London and the rest of the World State.

When Huxley was 16 and a student at the prestigious school Eton, an eye illness made him nearly blind. He recovered enough vision to go on to Oxford

University and graduate with honors, but not enough to fight in World War I, an important experience for many of his friends, or to do the scientific work he had dreamed of. Scientific ideas remained with him, however, and he used them in many of his books, particularly *Brave New World*. The idea of vision also remained important to him; his early novels contain scenes that seem ideal for motion pictures, and he later became a screenwriter.

He entered the literary world while he was at Oxford, meeting writers like Lytton Strachey and Bertrand Russell and becoming close friends with D.H. Lawrence, with whom you might think he had almost nothing in common.

Huxley published his first book, a collection of poems, in 1916. He married Maria Nys, a Belgian, in 1919. Their only child, Matthew Huxley, was born in 1920. The family divided their time between London and Europe, mostly Italy, in the 1920s, and traveled around the world in 1925 and 1926, seeing India and making a first visit to the United States.

Huxley liked the confidence, vitality, and "generous extravagance" he found in American life. But he wasn't so sure he liked the way vitality was expressed "in places of public amusement, in dancing and motoring . . . Nowhere, perhaps, is there so little conversation . . . It is all movement and noise, like the water gurgling out of a bath—down the waste. Yes, down the waste." Those thoughts of the actual world, from the book *Jesting Pilate*, were to color his picture of the perpetual happiness attempted in *Brave New World*.

His experiences in fascist Italy, where Benito Mussolini led an authoritarian government that fought against birth control in order to produce enough manpower for the next war, also provided materials for Huxley's bad Utopia, as did his reading of books critical of the Soviet Union.

Huxley wrote *Brave New World* in four months in 1931. It appeared three years after the publication of his best-seller, the novel *Point Counter Point*. During those three years, he had produced six books of stories, essays, poems, and plays, but nothing major. His biographer, Sybille Bedford, says, "It was time to produce some full-length fiction—he still felt like holding back from another straight novel—juggling in fiction form with the scientific possibilities of the future might be a new line."

Because *Brave New World* describes a bad Utopia, it is often compared with George Orwell's *1984*, another novel you may want to read, which also describes a possible horrible world of the future. The world of *1984* is one of tyranny, terror, and perpetual warfare. Orwell wrote it in 1948, shortly after the Allies had defeated Nazi Germany in World War II and just as the West was discovering the full dimensions of the evils of Soviet totalitarianism.

It's important to remember that Huxley wrote *Brave New World* in 1931, before Adolf Hitler came to power in Germany and before Joseph Stalin started the purges that killed millions of people in the Soviet Union. He therefore had no immediate real-life reason to make tyranny and terror major elements of his story. In 1958 Huxley himself said, "The future dictatorship of my imaginary world was a good deal less brutal than the future dictatorship so brilliantly portrayed by Orwell."

In 1937, the Huxleys came to the United States; in 1938 they went to Hollywood, where he became a screenwriter (among his films was an adaptation of Jane Austen's *Pride and Prejudice*, which starred the young Laurence Olivier). He remained for most of his life in California, and one of his novels caricatures what he saw as the strange life there: *After Many a Summer Dies the Swan*. In it the tycoon Jo Stoyte tries to achieve immortality through scientific experimentation, even if it means giving up humanity and returning to the completely animal state—an echo of *Brave New World*.

In 1946 Huxley wrote a Foreword to *Brave New World* in which he said he no longer wanted to make social sanity an impossibility, as he had in the novel. Though World War II had caused the deaths of some 20 million inhabitants of the Soviet Union, six million Jews, and millions of others, and the newly developed atomic bomb held the threat of even more extensive destruction, Huxley had become convinced that while still "rather rare," sanity could be achieved and said that he would like to see more of it. In the same year, he published *The Perennial Philosophy*, an anthology of texts with his own commentaries on mystical and religious approaches to a sane life in a sane society.

He also worried about the dangers that threatened sanity. In 1958, he published *Brave New World Revisited*, a set of essays on real-life problems and ideas you'll find in the novel—overpopulation, overorganization, and psychological techniques from salesmanship to hypnopaedia, or sleep-teaching. They're all tools that a government can abuse to deprive people of freedom, an abuse that Huxley wanted people to fight. If you want to further relate his bad new world to the real world, read *Brave New World Revisited*.

In the 1950s Huxley became famous for his interest in psychedelic or mind-expanding drugs like mescaline and LSD, which he apparently took a dozen times over ten years. Sybille Bedford says he was looking for a drug that would allow an escape from the self and that if taken with caution would be physically and socially harmless.

He put his beliefs in such a drug and in sanity into several books. Two, based on his experiences taking mescaline under supervision, were nonfiction: *Doors of Perception* (1954) and *Heaven and Hell* (1956). Some readers have read those books as encouragements to experiment freely with drugs, but Huxley warned of the dangers of such experiments in an appendix he wrote to *The Devils of Loudun* (1952), a psychological study of an episode in French history.

Another work centering on drugs and sanity was *Island* (1962), a novel that required 20 years of thought and five years of writing. Among other things, *Island* was an antidote to *Brave New World*, a good Utopia. Huxley deplored the drug he called *soma* in *Brave New World*—half tranquilizer, half intoxicant—which produces an artificial happiness that makes people content with their lack of freedom. He approved of the perfected version of LSD that the people of *Island* use in a religious way.

Huxley produced 47 books in his long career as a writer. The English critic Anthony Burgess has said that he equipped the novel with a brain. Other critics objected that he was a better essayist than novelist precisely because he cared more about his ideas than about plot or characters, and his novels' ideas often get in the way of the story.

But Huxley's emphasis on ideas and his skill as an essayist cannot hide one important fact: The books he wrote that are most read and best remembered today are all novels—*Crome Yellow*, *Antic Hay*, and *Point Counter Point* from the 1920s, *Brave New World* and *After Many a Summer Dies the Swan* from the 1930s. In

1959 the American Academy of Arts and Letters gave him the Award of Merit for the Novel, a prize given every five years; earlier recipients had been Ernest Hemingway, Thomas Mann, and Theodore Dreiser.

The range of Huxley's interests can be seen from his note that his "preliminary research" for *Island* included "Greek history, Polynesian anthropology, translations from Sanskrit and Chinese of Buddhist texts, scientific papers on pharmacology, neurophysiology, psychology and education, together with novels, poems, critical essays, travel books, political commentaries and conversations with all kinds of people, from philosophers to actresses, from patients in mental hospitals to tycoons in Rolls-Royces. . . ." He used similar, though probably fewer, sources for *Brave New World*.

This list gives you some perspective on the wide range of ideas that Huxley studied. He also wrote an early essay on ecology that helped inspire today's environmental movement. And he was a pacifist. This belief prevented him from becoming an American citizen because he would not say his pacifism was a matter of his religion, which might have made him an acceptable conscientious objector.

Huxley remained nearly blind all his life. Maria Huxley died in 1955, and Huxley married Laura Archera a year later. He died November 22, 1963, the same day that President John F. Kennedy was assassinated. He was cremated, and his ashes were buried in his parents' grave in England.

THE NOVEL

The Plot

Brave New World is partly a statement of ideas (expressed by characters with no more depth than cartoon characters) and only partly a story with a plot.

The first three chapters present most of the important ideas or themes of the novel. The Director of Hatcheries and Conditioning explains that this Utopia breeds people to order, artificially fertilizing a mother's eggs to create babies that grow in bottles. They are not born, but decanted. Everyone belongs to one of five classes, from the Alphas, the most intelligent, to the Epsilons, morons bred to do the dirty jobs that nobody else wants to do. The lower classes are multiplied by a budding process that can create up to 96 identical clones and produce over 15,000 brothers and sisters from a single ovary.

All the babies are conditioned, physically and chemically in the bottle, and psychologically after birth, to make them happy citizens of the society with both a liking and an aptitude for the work they will do. One psychological conditioning technique is hypnopaedia, or teaching people while they sleep—not teaching facts or analysis, but planting suggestions that will make people behave in certain ways. The Director also makes plain that sex is a source of happiness, a game people play with anyone who pleases them.

The Controller, one of the ten men who run the world, explains some of the more profound principles on which the Utopia is based. One is that "history is bunk"; the society limits people's knowledge of the past so they will not be able to compare the present with anything that might make them want to change the present. Another principle is that people should have no emotions, particularly no painful emotions; blind happiness is necessary for stability. One of the things that guarantees happiness is a drug called *soma*, which calms you down and gets you high but never gives you a hangover. Another is the "feelies," movies that reach your sense of touch as well as your sight and hearing.

After Huxley presents these themes in the first three chapters, the story begins. Bernard Marx, an Alpha of the top class, is on the verge of falling in love with Lenina Crowne, a woman who works in the Embryo Room of the Hatchery. Lenina has been dating Henry Foster, a Hatchery scientist; her friend Fanny nags her because she hasn't seen any other man for four months. Lenina likes Bernard but doesn't fall in love with him. Falling in love is a sin in this world in which one has sex with everyone else, and she is a happy, conforming citizen of the Utopia.

Bernard is neither happy nor conforming. He's a bit odd; for one thing, he's small for an Alpha, in a world where every member of the same caste is alike. He likes to treasure his differences from his fellows, but he lacks the courage to fight for his right to be an individual. In contrast is his friend Helmholtz Watson, successful in sports, sex, and community activities, but openly dissatisfied because instead of writing something beautiful and powerful, his job is to turn out propaganda.

Bernard attends a solidarity service of the Fordian religion, a parody of Christianity as practiced in England in the 1920s. It culminates in a sexual orgy, but he doesn't feel the true rapture experienced by the other 11 members of his group.

Bernard then takes Lenina to visit a Savage Reservation in North America. While signing his permit to go, the Director tells Bernard how he visited the same Reservation as a young man, taking a young woman from London who disappeared and was presumed dead. He then threatens Bernard with exile to Iceland because Bernard is a nonconformist: he doesn't gobble up pleasure in his leisure time like an infant.

At the Reservation, Bernard and Lenina meet John, a handsome young Savage who, Bernard soon realizes, is the son of the Director. Clearly, the woman the Director had taken to the Reservation long ago had become pregnant as the result of an accident that the citizens of Utopia would consider obscene. John has a fantasy picture of the Utopia from his mother's tales and a knowledge of Shakespeare that he mistakes for a guide to reality.

Bernard gets permission from the Controller to bring John and Linda, his mother, back to London. The Director had called a public meeting to announce Bernard's exile, but by greeting the Director as lover and father, respectively, Linda and John turn him into an obscene joke. Bernard stays and becomes the center of attention of all London because he is, in effect, John's guardian, and everybody wants to meet the Savage. Linda goes into a permanent *soma* trance after her years of exile on the Reservation. John is taken to see all the attractions of new world society and doesn't like them. But he enjoys arguing with Helmholtz about them, and about Shakespeare.

Lenina has become popular because she is thought to be sleeping with the Savage. Everyone envies her and wants to know what it's like. But, in fact, while she wants to sleep with John, he refuses because he, too, has fallen in love with her—and he has taken from Shakespeare the old-fashioned idea that lovers should be pure. Not understanding this, she finally comes to his apartment and takes her clothes off. He throws her out, calling her a prostitute because he thinks she's immoral, even though he wants her desperately.

John then learns that his mother is dying. The hospital illustrates the Utopia's approach to death, which includes trying to completely eliminate grief and pain. When John goes to visit Linda he is devastated; his display of grief frightens children being taught that death is a pleasant and natural process. John grows so angry that he tries to bring the Utopia back to what he considers sanity and morality by disrupting the daily distribution of *soma* to lower-caste Delta workers. That leads to a riot; John, Bernard, and Helmholtz are arrested.

The three then confront the Controller, who explains more of the Utopia's principles. Their conversation reveals that the Utopia achieves its happiness by giving up science, art, religion, and other things that we prize in the real world. The Controller sends Bernard to Iceland, after all, and Helmholtz to the Falkland Islands. He keeps John in England, but John finds a place where he can lead a hermit's life, complete with suffering. His solitude is invaded by Utopians who want to see him suffer, as though it were a sideshow spectacle; when Lenina joins the mob, he kills himself.

The Characters

Because this is a Utopian novel of ideas, few of the characters are three-dimensional people who come alive on the page. Most exist to voice ideas in words or to embody them in their behavior. John, Bernard, Helmholtz, and the Controller express ideas through real personalities, but you will enjoy most of the others more if you see them as cartoon characters rather than as full portraits that may seem so poorly drawn that they will disappoint you.

The Director of Hatcheries and Conditioning

The Director opens the novel by explaining the reproductive system of the brave new world, with genetically engineered babies growing in bottles. He loves to throw "scientific data" at his listeners so quickly that they can't understand them; he is a know-it-all impressed with his own importance. In fact, he knows less and is less important than the Controller, as you see when he is surprised that the Controller dares to talk about two forbidden topics—history and biological parents.

The Director comes alive only when he confesses to Bernard Marx that as a young man he went to a Savage Reservation, taking along a woman who disappeared there. She was pregnant with his baby, as a result of what the Utopia considers an obscene accident. The baby grows up to be John; his return to London leads to the total humiliation of the Director.

The Director's name is Thomas, but you learn this only because Linda, his onetime lover and John's mother, keeps referring to him as Tomakin.

Henry Foster

Henry is a scientist in the London Hatchery, an ideal citizen of the world state: efficient and intelligent at work, filling his leisure time with sports and casual sex. He is not an important character but helps Huxley explain the workings of the Hatchery, show Lenina's passionless sex life, and explore the gulf between Bernard and the "normal" citizens of Utopia.

Lenina Crowne

Lenina is young and pretty despite having lupus, an illness that causes reddish-brown blotches to appear on her skin. She is, like Henry Foster, a happy, shallow citizen, her one idiosyncracy is the fact that she sometimes spends more time than society approves dating one man exclusively.

Like all well-conditioned citizens of the World State, Lenina believes in having sex when she wants it. She can't understand that John avoids sex with her because he loves her and does not want to do something that he thinks—in his old-fashioned, part-Indian, part-Christian, part-Shakespearean way—will dishonor her. She embodies the conflict he feels between body and spirit, between love and lust.

Lenina is more a cartoon character than a real person, but she triggers John's emotional violence and provides the occasion for his suicide when she comes to see him whip himself.

The Controller, Mustapha Mond

Mond is one of the ten people who control the World State. He is good-natured and dedicated to his work, and extremely intelligent; he understands people and ideas that are different, which most Utopians cannot do. He has read such forbidden books as the works of Shakespeare and the Bible, and knows history and philosophy. Indeed, he resembles the Oxford professors that Huxley knew, and his discussion of happiness with the Savage resembles a tutorial between an Oxford don and his most challenging student.

Once a gifted scientist, the Controller made a conscious choice as a young man to become one of the rulers instead of a troublesome dissident. He is one of the few Utopians who can choose, who has free will, and this makes him more rounded and more attractive than most of the characters you'll meet in the book. It also makes him concerned with morality, but he uses his moral force and his sanity for the immoral and insane goals of the Utopia. You may decide that he is the most dangerous person in *Brave New World*.

Bernard Marx

A specialist in sleep-teaching, Bernard does not fit the uniformity that usually characterizes all members of the same caste. He is an Alpha of high intelligence and therefore a member of the elite, but he is small and therefore regarded as deformed. Other people speculate that too much alcohol was put into his bottle when he was still an embryo. He dislikes sports and likes to be alone, two very unusual traits among Utopians. When he first appears, he seems to dislike casual sex, another departure from the norm. He is unhappy in a world where everyone else is happy.

At first Bernard seems to take pleasure in his differentness, to like being a nonconformist and a rebel. Later, he reveals that his rebellion is less a matter of belief than of his own failure to be accepted. When he returns from the Savage Reservation with John, he is suddenly popular with important people and successful with women, and he loves it. Underneath, he has always wanted to be a happy member of the ruling class. In the end, he is exiled to Iceland and protests bitterly.

Helmholtz Watson

Helmholtz, like Bernard, is different from the average Alpha-plus intellectual. A mental giant who is also successful in sports and sex, he's almost too good to be true. But he is a nonconformist who knows that the world is capable of greater literature than the propaganda he writes so well—and that he is capable of producing it. When John the Savage introduces him to Shakespeare, Helmholtz only appreciates half of it; despite his genius, he's still limited by his Utopian upbringing. He remains willing to challenge society even if he can't change it, and accepts exile to the bleak Falkland Islands in the hope that physical discomfort and the company of other dissidents will stimulate his writing.

John the Savage

John is the son of two members of Utopia, but has grown up on a Savage Reservation. He is the only character who can really compare the two different worlds, and it is through him that Huxley shows that his Utopia is a bad one.

John's mother, Linda, became pregnant accidentally, a very unusual event in the brave new world. While she was pregnant, she visited a Savage Reservation, hurt herself in a fall, and got lost, missing her return trip to London. The Indians of the Reservation saved her life and she gave birth to John. The boy grew up absorbing three cultures: the Utopia he heard about from his mother; the Indian culture in which he lived, but which rejected him as an outsider; and the plays of Shakespeare, which he read in a book that survived from pre-Utopian days.

John, in short, is different from the other Savages and from the Utopians. He is tall and handsome, but much more of an alien in either world than Bernard is. John looks at both worlds through the lenses of the religion he acquired on the Reservation—a mixture of Christianity and American Indian beliefs—and the old-fashioned morality he learned from reading Shakespeare. His beliefs contradict those of the brave new world, as he shows in his struggle over sex with Lenina and his fight with the system after his mother dies. Eventually, the conflict is too much for him and he kills himself.

Linda

Linda is John's mother, a Beta minus who sleeps with the Director and becomes pregnant accidentally, 20 years before the action of the book begins. She falls while visiting a Savage Reservation, becomes unconscious, and remains lost until the Director has to leave. She is then rescued by Indians, gives birth to John, and lives for 20 years in the squalor of the Reservation, where she grows old, sick, and fat without the medical care that keeps people physically young in the Utopia. Behaving according to Utopian principles, she sleeps with many of the Indians on the Reservation and never understands why the women despise her or why the community makes John an outcast. When she returns to London, she takes ever-increasing doses of *soma* and stays perpetually high—until the drug kills her.

Other Elements

SETTING

Setting plays a particularly important role in *Brave New World*. Huxley's novel is a novel of Utopia, and a science-fiction novel. In both kinds of books the portrayal of individual characters tends to take a back seat to the portrayal of the society they live in. In some ways, the brave new world itself becomes the book's main character.

The story opens in London some 600 years in the future—632 A.F. (After Ford) in the calendar of the era. Centuries before, civilization as we know it was destroyed in the Nine Years' War. Out of the ruins grew the World State, an all-powerful government headed by ten World Controllers. Faith in Christ has been replaced by Faith in Ford, a mythologized version of Henry Ford, the auto pioneer who developed the mass production methods that have reached their zenith in the World State. Almost all traces of the past have been erased, for, as Henry Ford said, "History is bunk." Changing names show the changed society. Charing Cross, the London railroad station, is now Charing T Rocket Station: the cross has been supplanted by the T, from Henry Ford's Model T. Big Ben is now Big Henry. Westminster Abbey, one of England's most hallowed shrines, is now merely the site of a nightclub, the Westminster Abbey Cabaret.

The people of this world, born from test tubes and divided into five castes, are docile and happy, kept occupied by elaborate games like obstacle golf, entertainments like the "feelies," and sexual promiscuity. Disease is nonexistent, old age and death made as pleasant as possible so they can be ignored.

Some parts of the earth, however, are allowed to remain as they were before the World State came to power. With Bernard and Lenina, you visit one of these Savage Reservations, the New Mexican home of the Zuni Indians. It is a world away from civilized London: the Zunis are impoverished, dirty, ravaged by disease and old age, and still cling to their ancient religion.

The settings in *Brave New World*, then, seem to offer only the choice between civilized servitude and primitive ignorance and squalor. Are these the only choices available? One other is mentioned, the islands of exile—Iceland and the Falkland Islands—where malcontents like Bernard Marx and Helmholtz Watson are sent. But Huxley does not discuss these places in enough detail to let us know whether or not they provide any kind of alternative to the grim life he has presented in the rest of the book.

THEMES

This novel is about a Utopia, an ideal state—a bad ideal state. It is therefore a novel about ideas, and its themes are as important as its plot. They will be studied in depth in the chapter-by-chapter discussion of the book. Most are expressed as fundamental principles of the Utopia, the brave new world. Some come to light when one character, a Savage raised on an Indian reservation, confronts that world. As you find the themes, try to think not only about what they say about Huxley's Utopia, but also about Huxley's real world—and your own.

1. COMMUNITY, IDENTITY, STABILITY—VERSUS INDIVIDUAL FREEDOM

Community, Identity, Stability is the motto of the World State. It lists the Utopia's prime goals. Community is in part a result of identity and stability. It is also achieved through a religion that satirizes Christianity—a religion that encourages people to reach solidarity through sexual orgy. And it is achieved by organizing life so that a person is almost never alone.

Identity is in large part the result of genetic engineering. Society is divided into five classes or castes, hereditary social groups. In the lower three classes, people are cloned in order to produce up to 96 identical "twins." Identity is also achieved by teaching everyone to conform, so that someone who has or feels more than a minimum of individuality is made to feel different, odd, almost an outcast.

Stability is the third of the three goals, but it is the one the characters mention most often—the reason for designing society this way. The desire for stability, for instance, requires the production of large numbers of genetically identical "individuals," because people who are exactly the same are less likely to come into conflict. Stability means minimizing conflict, risk, and change.

2. SCIENCE AS A MEANS OF CONTROL

Brave New World is not only a Utopian book, it is also a science-fiction novel. But it does not predict much about science in general. Its theme "is the advancement of science as it affects human individuals," Huxley said in the Foreword he wrote in 1946, 15 years after he wrote the book. He did not focus on physical sciences like nuclear physics, though even in 1931 he knew that the production of nuclear energy (and weapons) was probable. He was more worried about dangers that appeared more obvious at that time—the possible misuse of biology, physiology, and psychology to achieve community, identity, and stability. Ironically, it becomes clear at the end of the book that the World State's complete control over human activity destroys even the scientific progress that gained it such control.

3. THE THREAT OF GENETIC ENGINEERING

Genetic engineering is a term that has come into use in recent years as scientists have learned to manipulate RNA and DNA, the proteins in every cell that determine the basic inherited characteristics of life. Huxley didn't use the phrase but he describes genetic engineering when he explains how his new world breeds prescribed numbers of humans artificially for specified qualities.

4. THE MISUSE OF PSYCHOLOGICAL CONDITIONING

Every human being in the new world is conditioned to fit society's needs—to like the work he will have to do. Human embryos do not grow inside their mothers' wombs but in bottles. Biological or physiological conditioning consists of adding chemicals or spinning the bottles to prepare the embryos for the levels of strength, intelligence, and aptitude required for given jobs. After they are "decanted" from the bottles, people are psychologically conditioned, mainly by hypnopaedia or sleep-teaching. You might say that at every stage the society brainwashes its citizens.

5. THE PURSUIT OF HAPPINESS CARRIED TO AN EXTREME

A society can achieve stability only when everyone is happy, and the brave new world tries hard to ensure that every person *is* happy. It does its best to eliminate any painful emotion, which means every deep feeling, every passion. It uses genetic engineering and conditioning to ensure that everyone is happy with his or her work.

6. THE CHEAPENING OF SEXUAL PLEASURE

Sex is a primary source of happiness. The brave new world makes promiscuity a virtue: you have sex with any partner you want, who wants you—and sooner or later every partner will want you. (As a child, you learn in your sleep that "everyone belongs to everyone else.") In this Utopia, what we think of as true love for one person would lead to neurotic passions and the establishment of family life, both of which would interfere with community and stability. Nobody is allowed to become pregnant because nobody is born, only decanted from a bottle. Many females are born sterile by design; those who are not are trained by "Malthusian drill" to use contraceptives properly.

7. THE PURSUIT OF HAPPINESS THROUGH DRUGS

Soma is a drug used by everyone in the brave new world. It calms people and gets them high at the same time, but without hangovers or nasty side effects. The rulers of the brave new world had put 2000 pharmacologists and biochemists to work long before the action of the novel begins; in six years they had perfected the drug. Huxley believed in the possibility of a drug that would enable people to escape from themselves and help them achieve knowledge of God, but he made *soma* a parody and degradation of that possibility.

8. THE THREAT OF MINDLESS CONSUMPTION AND MINDLESS DIVERSIONS

This society offers its members distractions that they must enjoy in common—never alone—because solitude breeds instability. Huxley mentions but never explains sports that use complex equipment whose manufacture keeps the economy rolling—sports called Obstacle Golf and Centrifugal Bumble-puppy. But the chief emblem of *Brave New World* is the Feelies—movies that feature not only sight and sound but also the sensation of touch, so that when people watch a couple making love on a bearskin rug, they can feel every hair of the bear on their own bodies.

9. THE DESTRUCTION OF THE FAMILY

The combination of genetic engineering, bottle-birth, and sexual promiscuity means there is no monogamy, marriage, or family. "Mother" and "father" are obscene words that may be used scientifically on rare, carefully chosen occasions to label ancient sources of psychological problems.

10. THE DENIAL OF DEATH

The brave new world insists that death is a natural and not unpleasant process. There is no old age or visible senility. Children are conditioned at hospitals for the dying and given sweets to eat when they hear of death occurring. This conditioning does not—as it might—prepare people to cope with the death of a loved one or with their own mortality. It eliminates the painful emotions of grief and loss, and the spiritual significance of death, which Huxley made increasingly important in his later novels.

11. THE OPPRESSION OF INDIVIDUAL DIFFERENCES

Some characters in *Brave New World* differ from the norm. Bernard is small for an Alpha and fond of solitude; Helmholtz, though seemingly "every centimetre an Alpha-Plus," knows he is too intelligent for the work he performs; John the Savage, genetically a member of the World State, has never been properly conditioned to become a citizen of it. Even the Controller, Mustapha Mond, stands apart because of his leadership abilities. Yet in each case these differences are crushed: Bernard and Helmholtz are exiled; John commits suicide; and the Mond stifles his own individuality in exchange for the power he wields as Controller. What does this say about Huxley's Utopia?

11. WHAT DOES SUCH A SYSTEM COST?

This Utopia has a good side: there is no war or poverty, little disease or social unrest. But Huxley keeps asking, what does society have to pay for these benefits? The price, he makes clear, is high. The first clue is in the epigraph, the quotation at the front of the book. It is in French, but written by a Russian, Nicolas Berdiaeff. It says, "Utopias appear to be much easier to realize than one formerly believed. We currently face a question that would otherwise fill us with anguish: How to avoid their becoming definitively real?"

By the time you hear the conversation between the Controller, one of the men who runs the new world, and John, the Savage, you've learned that citizens of this Utopia must give up love, family, science, art, religion, and history. At the end of the book, John commits suicide and you see that the price of this brave new world is fatally high.

STYLE

Although Huxley's writing style makes him easy to read, his complex ideas make readers think. Even if you're not familiar with his vocabulary or philosophy, you can see that, as the critic Laurence Brander says, "The prose was witty and ran clearly and nimbly."

Huxley's witty, clear, nimble prose is very much an upper-class tradition. *Brave New World*—like all of Huxley's novels—is a novel of ideas, which means that the characters must have ideas and must be able to express them eloquently and cleverly. This demands that the author have considerable knowledge. In pre-World War II England such novels were more likely to have been written by members of the upper class, simply because they had much greater access to good education. Huxley, we remember, attended Eton and Oxford.

Huxley, like other upper-class Englishmen, was familiar with history and literature. He expected his readers to know the plays of Shakespeare, to recognize names like Malthus and Marx, to be comfortable with a word like "predestination." (Literally "predestine" means only "to determine in advance," but it is most importantly a word from Christian theology—describing, in one version, the doctrine that God knows in advance everything that will ever happen, and thereby decides who will be saved and who will be damned.)

Although Huxley was very serious about ideas, he never stopped seeing their humorous possibilities. His biographer, Sybille Bedford, says that in 1946 he gave the commencement speech at a progressive school in California, where he urged the students *not* to imitate "the young man of that ancient limerick... who

. . . . said "Damn,
It is borne in on me that I am
  A creature that moves
  In predestinate grooves;
I'm not even a bus, I'm a tram!"

To appreciate this joke, you have to remember how a tram or trolley car moves on its tracks. It's a reminder that you'll have much more fun with *Brave New World* and get much more out of it if you don't let the language scare or bore you. Use the glossary in this guide and your dictionary as tools. See how many of the words you know. See if you can guess what some words mean from their spelling and the context in which you find them. Look them up and see how close you are. Look up the ones whose meaning you can't guess. If you put even a few of the words you meet for the first time in *Brave New World* into your vocabulary, you'll be winning a great game.

Games were an important part of an upper-class English education in Huxley's day. Many elite students developed a readiness to make jokes with words and ideas. You may find some of Huxley's jokes funny, while you may think the humor has vanished from others. But you'll have more fun with the book if you try to spot the humor. You'll find big jokes like the Feelies, movies that you can feel, as well as see and hear. You'll also find little jokes like plays on words—as in calling the process for getting a baby out of its bottle "decanting," a word ordinarily used only for fine wine. There is humor in "orgy-porgy," a combination of religious ritual and group sex, a parody of a child's nursery rhyme.

In *Brave New World* Huxley plays many games with his characters' names. He turns *Our Lord* into *Our Ford,* for Henry Ford, the inventor of the modern assembly line and the cheap cars that embodied the machine age for the average man. He names one of his main characters for Karl Marx, the father of the ideas of Communism. His heroine is called Lenina, after the man who led the Russian Revolution. Benito Hoover, a minor character, has the first name of the dictator of fascist Italy and the last name of the President of the United States who led the nation into the Great Depression, but he is "notoriously good-natured." Look up any names you don't recognize.

POINT OF VIEW

Huxley's point of view in *Brave New World* is third person, omniscient (all-knowing). The narrator is not one of the characters and therefore has the ability to tell us what is going on within any of the characters' minds. This ability is particularly useful in showing us a cross section of this strange society of the future. We're able to be with the Director of Hatcheries and Conditioning in the Central London Conditioning and Hatchery Centre, with Lenina Crowne at the Westminster Abbey Cabaret, with Bernard Marx at the Fordson Community Singery. The technique reaches an extreme in Chapter Three, when we hear a babble of unidentified voices—Lenina's, Fanny Crowne's, Mustapha Mond's—that at first sound chaotic but soon give us a vivid understanding of this brave new world.

FORM AND STRUCTURE

Brave New World fits into a long tradition of books about Utopia, an ideal state where everything is done for the good of humanity as a whole, and evils like war and poverty cannot exist.

The word "Utopia" means "no place" in Greek. Sir Thomas More first used it in 1516 as the title of a book about such an ideal state. But the idea of a Utopia goes much further back. Many critics consider Plato's *Republic,* written in the fourth century B.C., a Utopian book.

"Utopia" came to have a second meaning soon after Sir Thomas More used it—"an impractical scheme for social improvement." The idea that Utopias are silly and impractical helped make them a subject for satire, a kind of literature that makes fun of something, exposing wickedness and foolishness through wit and irony. (Irony is the use of words to express an idea that is the direct opposite of the stated meaning, or an outcome of events contrary to what was expected.)

In this way two Utopian traditions developed in English literature. One was optimistic and idealistic—like More's, or Edward Bellamy's *Looking Backward* (1888), which foresaw a mildly socialist, perfect state. H.G. Wells, an important English writer, believed in progress through science and wrote both novels and nonfiction about social and scientific changes that could produce a Utopia.

The second tradition was satiric, like Jonathan Swift's *Gulliver's Travels* (1726), in which both tiny and gigantic residents of distant lands were used to satirize the England of Swift's day. Another satiric Utopia was Samuel Butler's *Erewhon* (1872; the title is an anagram of "nowhere"), which made crime a disease to be cured and disease a crime to be punished.

In *Brave New World*, Huxley clearly belongs in the satiric group. (Though toward the end of his career he wrote a nonsatiric novel of a good Utopia, *Island*.) He told a friend that he started to write *Brave New World* as a satire on the works of H.G. Wells. Soon he increased his targets, making fun not only of science but also of religion, using his idea of the future to attack the present.

As in most works about Utopia, *Brave New World* lacks the complexity of characterization that marks other kinds of great novels. The people tend to represent ideas the author likes or dislikes. Few are three-dimensional or true to life; most resemble cartoon characters. As do many writers of Utopian works, Huxley brings in an outsider (John the Savage) who can see the flaws of the society that are invisible to those who have grown up within it.

As Huxley worked on his book, his satire darkened. The book became a serious warning that if we use science as an instrument of power, we will probably apply it to human beings in the wrong way, producing a horrible society. *Brave New World* belongs firmly in the tradition of Utopian writing, but the Utopia it portrays is a bleak one, indeed.

The Story

CHAPTER ONE

The novel begins by plunging you into a world you can't quite recognize: it's familiar but there's something wrong, or at least different from what you're used to. For example, it starts like a movie, with a long shot of a building—but a "squat" building "only" thirty-four stories high. The building bears a name unlike any you've heard in real life—"Central London Hatchery and Conditioning Centre"—and the motto of a World State you know doesn't exist.

The camera's eye then moves through a north window into the cold Fertilizing Room, and focuses on someone you know is a very important person from the way he speaks. He is the Director of Hatcheries and Conditioning, and he's explaining things to a group of new students who still have only a very limited understanding of what goes on here.

You may find the Director and his Hatchery strange, but you probably know how the students feel as they try to note everything the Director says, even his opening remark, "Begin at the beginning." You know how anxious you can be to make sure you don't miss something a teacher says, something that will be important later on.

In fact, the functions of the Hatchery are hard to understand because Huxley has the Director throw large amounts of "scientific data" at you without giving you time to figure out their meaning. Huxley thereby undermines one of his intentions here—to use the Director as a cartoon character who expounds some of the scientific ideas that the author wants you to think about. He also wants to satirize a world that makes such a know-it-all important and powerful.

Sometimes the real world gives such people power, too. You may meet scientists like the Director in college or businesspeople like him at work.

The Director talks about incubators and fertilizing, about surgically removing the ovary from the female and keeping it alive artificially. He talks about bringing together ova (the unfertilized eggs of a female) and male gametes (the cells or spermatozoa containing the father's half of the genetic material needed to make a new being) in a glass container. He talks about a mysterious budding process that turns one egg into 96 embryos. The Director mentions all these things and more before Huxley tells you that the Hatchery hatches human beings.

The Director takes that fact for granted, but Huxley surprises you all the more by letting it sneak up on you. Do you think it's frightening or disgusting to breed human beings like chickens on a farm? In this Utopia, the price is worth paying to control the total population; it breeds as many or as few people as the world controllers decide are needed. Huxley's imaginary world is thus dealing with a real world problem—overpopulation. You've probably read or heard warnings about this, warnings that the world, or the United States, or a developing country like Kenya, has more people than it can feed. China is trying to reward families that have only one child and penalize those that have more, but no country has yet tried to do what Huxley's brave new world does.

The Director talks less about stemming overpopulation than he does about increasing population in the right way. In the real world, it's unusual for a woman to produce more than ten children, and the average American family has two or fewer. In Huxley's world, Bokanovsky's budding process and Podsnap's ripening technique can produce over 15,000 brothers and sisters from a single ovary. You may know this idea from the word "cloning," used in science fiction and to describe look-alike clothing styles. Identical clones will make a stable community, the Director says, one without conflict.

In the world of Bokanovsky and Podsnap, babies are not born. They develop in bottles and are "decanted"—a word that usually refers to pouring wine gently out of its bottle so that the sediment at the bottom is not disturbed.

The Director takes you and the students to the bottling room, where you learn that the clone-embryo grows inside the bottle on a bed of sow's peritoneum (the lining of the abdomen of an adult female pig). In the embryo room, the bottled embryos move slowly on belts that travel over three tiers of racks—a total of 2136 meters (about 1⅓ miles) during the 267 days before decanting. Huxley makes a point of the distance because each meter represents a point at which the embryo is given specific conditioning for its future life.

The 267 days are approximately equal to the nine months it takes a baby to develop inside its mother in the real world, but neither Director nor students mention that kind of birth. "Mother" is an unmentionable and obscene word in this brave new world, as you'll see in the next chapter. Although Huxley doesn't state it yet, if you think about it you'll see that bokanovskifying and bottling mean that nobody becomes pregnant. This gives you a hint of what will be said concerning sex and family life.

In this world, a person's class status is biologically and chemically engineered. The genes that determine brains and brawn are carefully selected. Then, a bottled embryo undergoes the initial conditioning that will determine its skills and strength, in keeping with its destiny as an Alpha, Beta, Gamma, Delta, or Epsilon.

These names are letters in the Greek alphabet, familiar to Huxley's original English readers because in English schools they are used as grades—like our As, Bs, etc.—with Alpha plus the best and Epsilon minus the worst. In *Brave New World*, each names a class or caste. Alphas and Betas remain individuals; only Gammas, Deltas, and Epsilons are bokanovskified. Alpha embryos receive the most oxygen in order to develop the best brains; Epsilons receive the least because they won't need intelligence for the work they'll do, like shoveling sewage.

Embryos predestined to be tropical workers are inoculated against typhoid and sleeping sickness. Bottles containing future astronauts are kept constantly in rotation to improve their sense of balance. There's a conditioning routine for every function in this society. Nobody complains about having to do hard, dirty, or boring work; everyone is conditioned to do their job well and to like it.

In this chapter you meet two people besides the Director, though you hardly notice them in the barrage of scientific information, and you don't get to know them very well until later. One is Henry Foster, a Hatchery scientist, one of the cardboard characters that Huxley pushes to keep the plot moving. The other is Lenina Crowne, one of only two women who are important in the story. She is as close as *Brave New World* comes to having a heroine, but she is so completely a creature of the system that she barely has any personality. She is a technician in the embryo room, which like a photographic darkroom can be lit only with red light. Everybody who works in this room has purple eyes and lupus, a disease that causes large red or brown patches to appear on the skin. Huxley doesn't tell you whether this is a result of the red light or a way of matching the workers to the workplace, but neither purple eyes nor blotched skin prevents Lenina from being "uncommonly pretty." Thus, the author shows you that standards of beauty and sex appeal are different in this world of the future.

NOTE: *Brave New World* is a novel about a Utopia, an ideal state in which everything is done for the good of humanity, and evils like poverty and war cannot exist.

Perhaps you, too, have created stories about imaginary countries in which everything happens the way you think it should, countries that could be called ideal states if you looked at them closely. Or you may have seen the television program, "Fantasy Island," which is a modern, mass-audience twist on the theme of Utopia, a place that grants you your fondest wishes.

Some aspects of *Brave New World* may seem attractive to you. Everybody is happy, hygienic, and economically secure. There is little sickness and no old age, poverty, crime, or war. But notice how the Director emphasizes that bokanovskifying is "one of the major instruments of social stability," and how he reminds his students that the motto of the World State is "Community, Identity, Stability."

The most important events in this novel all center around conflicts between people like the Director, who want to maintain stability, and people whose actions might threaten this stability, even unintentionally. The Director never questions what people have to give up to achieve the World State's goals. Later in the book, other characters do ask this question, and they provide some answers. As you read *Brave New World,* keep asking yourself this question. What price would we have to pay to live in this Utopia?

CHAPTER TWO

This chapter takes you from the biological and chemical conditioning of embryos to the psychological conditioning of children in Huxley's world of the future. The Director shows the students how Delta infants, color-coded in khaki clothes, crawl naturally toward picture books and real flowers, only to be terrorized by the noises of explosions, bells, and sirens and then traumatized by electric shock. The babies learn to associate books and flowers with those painful experiences, and turn away from them.

NOTE: This section of the center is named the Neo-Pavlovian Conditioning Rooms for the Russian scientist, Ivan Petrovich Pavlov (1849–1936). In a classic experiment he trained dogs to salivate at the sound of a bell that was linked to memories of food, proving the theory of the conditioned reflex. You'll see how Pavlov's theories have been used—and misused—throughout the brave new world.

The reason for making the infants dislike books is psychological—if they read the wrong things, they might lose a bit of the conditioning that guarantees stability. The reason for making them dislike flowers is economic. If, as adults, they traveled to the country, they would "consume transport." Here Huxley makes fun of the way some economists use the word "consume." He means that when they travel to the country, people use cars, trains, or helicopters. Thus, "consuming transport" is good for an economy that sells transport services and makes vehicles. But if they only went to enjoy nature, they would "consume" nothing else. Instead, they are conditioned to dislike nature and love sports, which have been redesigned to involve elaborate mechanical and electronic equipment. They therefore "consume" transport in traveling to the country to "consume" sports equipment. This sounds as though they gobble it up, but in reality they are using it and wearing it out, thereby doubling the economic benefit.

In proceeding to the next kind of conditioning, the Director gives you your first clue to this world's religion: the phrase "Our Ford," obviously used as religious people in the real world might say "Our Lord." You learn that the calendar year is no longer A.D. (Anno Domini, the year of our Lord) but A.F., After Ford. Instead of making the sign of the cross, the Director makes the sign of the T, from the Model T Ford.

NOTE: This is a parody of Christianity—not so much of its essential beliefs as of the way organized religion can be used to control society. In 1931 it seemed funnier and more daring than it does today, especially in England, where the Anglican church is established (linked to the state). Huxley made Ford the new Jesus because Ford became the best-known symbol of modern industry after he invented the automobile assembly line that produced cheap, basically identical cars. Watch for further elaboration of the Ford religion in later chapters.

The next conditioning technique is hypnopaedia, sleep-teaching. The Director tells the students it was discovered accidentally hundreds of years earlier by a little Polish boy who lived with his "father" and "mother," two words that hit the students' ears with much more force than obscene words hit your ears today. Would you be shocked if your high school principal, a middle-aged gentleman who spoke correct English with a proper accent, used a carefully enunciated obscene word during a school assembly? That's how the students feel when the Director utters those unmentionable words.

In the Director's story, little Reuben Rabinovitch discovered hypnopaedia by hearing in his sleep a broadcast by George Bernard Shaw, the British dramatist, and sleep-learning it by heart though he knew no English. Shaw thought himself a genius both as playwright and political thinker, as did many of his followers. Huxley makes a little joke at the expense of people who claim to recognize genius but really know no more about it than a sleeping child who can't speak the language it's expressed in.

The Director goes on to explain that hypnopaedia doesn't work for teaching facts or analysis. It works only for "moral education," which here means conditioning people's behavior by verbal suggestion when their psychological resistance is low—by repeated messages about what's good or bad, in words that require no intellectual activity but can be digested by a sleeping brain. (This is Huxley's own explanation in *Brave New World Revisited,* a book of essays written in 1958, a generation after the novel appeared. He also found that in the real world, sleep-teaching of both kinds shows mixed results.)

The Director gives you and the students an example of this kind of moral education, a sleep-lesson in class consciousness for Betas. They learn to love being Betas, to respect Alphas who "work much harder than we do, because they're so frightfully clever," and to be glad they're not Gammas, Deltas, or Epsilons, each more stupid than the preceding. "Oh no," the tape suggests to them, "I *don't* want to play with Delta children."

In other words, the Betas learn to love the system and their place in it. The lesson, repeated 120 times in each of three sessions a week for 30 months, seals them into that place. Huxley likens it to drops of liquid sealing wax, which the English upper classes used to seal envelopes, placing a drop of wax on the edge of the flap and pressing a design into it as the wax hardened. The envelope couldn't be opened without showing a break in the wax. Sealing wax is seen infrequently in the U.S. today, but if you imagine a candle dripping endlessly, you will understand the effect.

CHAPTER THREE

This chapter switches back and forth from place to place and from one set of characters to another in order to give you your first view of sex, love, and the nonexistent family in the brave new world.

In the first scene, the Director and some almost embarrassed students show you that sex is a game that children are encouraged to play. Later scenes make plain that for adults, sex is a wholesome source of happiness, rather like going to a health club. Nobody lives with or is married to one person at a time. In fact, there is no marriage. Everybody is expected to be promiscuous—to keep switching sexual partners without any important reason for distinguishing one partner from another.

Huxley expected his readers to be surprised or at least to giggle at the idea of promiscuity as a virtue. Some of them surely thought promiscuity meant happiness, as Huxley's characters do, but they had grown up with the idea that it was wicked. Today, many teachers and clergymen claim that high school and college students are promiscuous, but *Time* magazine says that Americans in general are becoming less so. "Promiscuous" is a word that can make you feel a connection between the real world and *Brave New World*, and help you decide if you would like the novel's world better than the one you live in.

In the first scene, the Director is upstaged by one of the ten men who run the world, the Resident Controller for Western Europe, Mustapha Mond. (Alfred Mond was a British chemist, economist, and cabinet minister; for Huxley's original readers the name probably had the same kind of ring that "Rashid Rockefeller" would for Americans.) He tells the students, "History is bunk." This is an anti-intellectual quotation from Henry Ford, who believed that a person who wasted time studying history would never create anything as revolutionary as an assembly line. But the Resident Controllers tell people that "history is bunk" for another reason: people who know history can compare the present with the past. They know the world can change, and that knowledge is a threat to stability. (George Orwell went a step further in *1984* and had the rulers of his state constantly rewrite history because they knew that if they controlled people's memories of the past, it would be easier to control the present.) This quote allows Huxley to list the glories of history, from the Bible to Beethoven, in a single paragraph, thus showing what his new world has whisked away like dust.

Also whisked away is the family. The Controller's description of traditional families links fathers with misery, mothers with perversion, brothers and sisters with madness and suicide.

Mond says this is the wisdom of Our Freud, as Our Ford chose "for some inscrutable reason . . . to call himself whenever he spoke of psychological matters." This is another of the intellectual and serious jokes that Huxley loves to make. Sigmund Freud revolutionized psychology and invented psychoanalysis, but people misuse his name and twist his ideas to fit their dogmas, just as they do Christ's.

Mond compares love to a pipe full of water that jets forth dangerously if you make just one hole in it. This is a metaphor for individual motherhood and monogamy, which he believes produces people who are mad (meaning "insane," not "angry"), wicked, and miserable. The water only makes safe, "piddling little fountains" if you put many holes in the pipe—a metaphor for the safety of growing up in a group and for being promiscuous.

After the Controller repeats the Director's lessons about the need for stability and population control, he adds something new—the elimination of emotions, particularly painful emotions. When he asks the students if they've ever experienced a painful feeling, one says it was "horrible" when a girl made him wait nearly four weeks before going to bed with him. Do you think that's real pain? Or is it part of Huxley's satire?

NOTE: Even as satire, this idea is very important in Huxley's book: the idea that people can live happily without emotional pain, and that the way to achieve this happiness is to eliminate as many emotions as possible, because even happy feelings carry the possibility of pain with them. Huxley's Utopia is built on this idea. Do you think it's true that human beings can live this way? Would it make you happy in the long run? Make a note of your answer so you can see if you change your mind after you finish the book.

The Controller makes these points as the "camera eye" of the novel switches back and forth from him to Lenina Crowne coming off work, changing clothes, and talking to her friend Fanny; from them to Henry Foster and other men, and back again. As the chapter continues, it becomes more and more difficult to tell which scene you're viewing because Huxley stops identifying the character who is speaking at any given moment, and you have to decide that from the nature of the remark.

Through Lenina and Fanny you learn more of the mechanics of feeling good, as they turn different taps for different perfumes and use a "vibro-vacuum" for toning up skin and muscles. In a world where no woman bears a child, women need periodic Pregnancy Substitutes—chemical pills and injections to give them the hormonal benefits that pregnancy would give their bodies. And one fashion item is a "Malthusian belt" loaded with contraceptives, rather like a soldier's bandolier with magazines of bullets. Thomas Malthus was a political economist who wrote in 1798 that population increases much more rapidly than does subsistence; later groups that wanted to limit population often invoked his name.

The two women also give you a closer look than the Controller's talk did at personal relations in a world that prizes promiscuity and makes monogamy impossible. Fanny reproaches Lenina for seeing nobody but

Henry Foster for four months. She calls Henry a "perfect gentleman" *because* he has other girlfriends at the same time.

After the scene switches to Henry, you meet another very important character: Bernard Marx, a specialist in hypnopaedia. He's unusual in this world because he likes to be alone, and he despises Foster for conforming to the culture of promiscuity, drugs, and "feelies"—movies that appeal not only to your eyes and ears but also to your sense of touch. (*Brave New World* was written only a few years after silent films gave way to "talkies," as the first films in which audiences could hear the actors speak were called.)

Bernard is on the verge of falling in love with Lenina, and he hates Foster for talking about her as though she were a piece of meat. Lenina is also interested in Bernard, if only because he is a bit *different* in a world in which everybody conforms. Bernard is physically small for an Alpha, and Fanny repeats a rumor that his small stature was caused by someone adding too much alcohol to his blood-surrogate when he was an embryo. Lenina says "What nonsense," but later she'll wonder if this is true.

NOTE: When Bernard becomes angry, Foster offers him a tablet of *soma*. Although this is one of the most important concepts in the book, Huxley doesn't signal it for you the first time he mentions it. A voice that can only be that of the Controller reviewing the history that produced the world state, says that five centuries earlier the rulers realized the need for the perfect drug. They put 2000 pharmacologists and biochemists to work, and in six years they produced the drug. The voice doesn't mention the name *soma*; Foster does that when he offers Bernard the tablet, and Foster's friend the Assistant Predestinator says, "One cubic centimetre cures ten gloomy sentiments." A bit later, the Controller says that half a gram of *soma* is the same as a half-holiday, a gram equals a weekend, "two grams for a trip to the gorgeous East, three for a dark eternity on the Moon." In other words, *soma* makes you high—like marijuana or LSD—but has none of the dangerous side effects those drugs can have. This world couldn't function without *soma*, because the world can't be kept free of pain without a drug that tranquilizes people and makes them high at the same time—and never leaves them with hangovers.

The word *soma*, which Huxley always puts in italics, is from the Sanskrit language of ancient India. It refers to both an intoxicating drink used in the Vedic religious rituals there and the plant from whose juice the drink was made—a plant whose true identity we don't know. *Soma* is also the Greek word for body, and can be found in the English word "somatic," an adjective meaning "of the body, as distinct from the mind." Huxley probably enjoyed his trilingual pun.

The Controller's description of *soma* is part of a scene scattered over several paragraphs in which he explains that in this Utopia there is no old age. People remain physiologically young until they reach their sixties and die. Would you like to stay young and healthy until you die, and know that you would die in your sixties? Many people would say "yes" at first. But what price would you have to pay for a lifetime of youth? Huxley wants you to answer that question, too. If you never grow old, you never feel the pains of aging—but you never feel the positive emotions of achievement or contentment with the life you've lived, either. You never know the wisdom that comes from changes in your body, mind, and life, from the knowledge that death is approaching.

CHAPTER FOUR

In this chapter, Huxley turns from building up his new-world technology to telling his story, which gives more vivid life to Lenina, Bernard, and a new character named Helmholtz Watson. Lenina is still little more than the typical hedonist of the new world. (A hedonist is someone who believes that pleasure is the highest good.) In the first scene, Lenina makes sexual advances toward Bernard in a crowded elevator and can't understand why he is embarrassed. Then she goes to a suburban park with Henry Foster to "consume" sports equipment. In some ways she is the book's heroine, but Huxley forces you to see how shallow she is.

In the second scene, Bernard reveals himself as someone you can understand more easily than most of the other characters you have met so far—because he's more of an individual, more like you or someone you know, and less like the instructional cartoon characters of the Director and Controller or the always cheerful conformists and clones.

By accident, Bernard is small for an Alpha. This makes it hard for him to deal with members of lower castes, who are as small as he is, but by design. He treats them in the arrogant but insecure way that some poor whites in the old South treated blacks, or that lower-class British people treated natives in Africa or India in the days of the British Empire. Huxley's original readers knew such people as friends or relations, or through the novels of Rudyard Kipling. Americans might know them best through the novels of William Faulkner.

Bernard goes to meet his friend Helmholtz, a writer and emotional engineer. Like Bernard, Helmholtz is unhappy in a world of people who are always happy.

Like Bernard, he is different from most Alphas. He is different not because he is short and feels inadequate, but because he is a mental giant. He is successful in sports, sex, and community activities—all the activities in which Bernard feels he is a failure. But Helmholtz is still not happy because he knows he is capable of writing something beautiful and powerful, rather than the nonsense that he has to write for the press or the feelies.

While the two friends are talking, Bernard suddenly suspects someone is spying on them, flings the door open, and finds nobody there. This is surprising, because while you've been told that the state runs everything in this new world, you haven't felt oppressed by the rulers. You find nothing like the Big Brother of George Orwell's novel *1984* or the secret police in books about Nazi Germany or the Soviet Union. The scene is a reminder that this world, too, is a dictatorship.

CHAPTER FIVE

This chapter gives more dimensions to the familiar pictures of Lenina as hedonist and well-trained citizen and Bernard as a malcontent among contented comrades. In scene one, Lenina and Henry return from their Obstacle Golf game. By now you know that Huxley has a reason, which will be revealed in a later chapter, for scattering bits of technological and ideological information along their path—like Henry's telling Lenina that the dead are all cremated so the new world can recover the phosphorus from their bodies. They have dinner and go to a nightclub in what was Westminster Abbey 600 years earlier. There they listen to a kind of electronic pop music that might describe what rock musicians play on Moog synthesizers 50 years after the book was written.

They get high on *soma* and go up to Henry's room for a night of sex. Lenina is so well conditioned that despite her high, she takes all the contraceptive precautions she learned in the Malthusian drill she performed three times a week, every week for six years of her teens. Huxley uses Lenina to underline the point that pregnancy is a sin, a crime, and a disgusting ailment in the world of Hatcheries, and that it almost never happens.

Scene two switches to Bernard, who attends a solidarity service, the equivalent of a religious service, where he reveals new dimensions of his difference from other brave new worldlings, and of his unhappiness. The new world version of a church is a Community Singery. The one Bernard attends is a skyscraper on the site a Londoner would know as St. Paul's Cathedral.

Every solidarity service takes place in a group of twelve people, six men and six women who sit in a circle, sing twelve-stanza hymns, and take a communion of solid and liquid *soma* instead of wafers and wine. The participants all go into a religious frenzy—except for Bernard, who doesn't really feel the ecstacy, but pretends to.

The frenzy takes the members of the group into a dance and the song that is one of the most remembered bits of this book, the parody of a nursery rhyme:

Orgy-porgy, Ford and fun,
Kiss the girls and make them One.
Boys at one with girls at peace;
Orgy-porgy gives release.

The group then does indeed fall "in partial disintegration" into a real orgy, though it seems to be by couples rather than group sex.

Even that doesn't give Bernard the experience of true rapture that his partners seem to feel. Huxley underlines that this rapture is not the same as excitement, because if you're excited, you're still not satisfied. This feeling is satisfying. Bernard is miserable that he has not achieved it, and thinks the failure must have been his own fault.

In this scene, Huxley satirizes both religion and sex, but still shows how both serve one of the goals of the brave new world, Community.

CHAPTER SIX

Lenina and Bernard get together in this chapter, and travel from England to North America to visit a Savage Reservation that is not unlike today's Indian reservations. Huxley signals that he is bringing you a step closer to a climax by stressing that he is taking you and his characters to a place with none of the endless, emotionless pleasures of this Utopia, a place with no running perfume, no television, "no hot water even."

Lenina is troubled because she thinks Bernard is odd, and she wonders if what she once called "Nonsense" might be true—that he was given too much alcohol while he was still an embryo in a bottle. He's odd because he hates crowds and wants to be alone with her even when they aren't making love. He's odd because he'd rather take a walk in England's beautiful Lake District than fly to Amsterdam and see the women's heavyweight wrestling championship. He's odd because he wants to look at a stormy sea without listening to sugary music on the radio. Most of all he's odd because he is capable of wishing he was free rather than enslaved by his conditioning.

But Bernard doesn't do many of the things he wants to do. He's odd in his desires but not in his behavior. In the end he does just what a brave new worldling should do: he leaves the choppy waters of the English channel, flies Lenina home in his helicopter, takes four tablets of *soma* at a gulp, and goes to bed with her.

The next day Bernard finds that even he, like Henry Foster, can think of Lenina as a piece of meat. He hates that, but he realizes that she likes thinking of herself that way. That doesn't stop him from returning to his odd desires: he tells her he wants to feel something strongly, passionately. He wants to be an adult, to be capable of waiting for pleasure, instead of an infant who must have his pleasure right now.

Lenina is disturbed by this, so disturbed that she thinks, "Perhaps he had found her too plump, after all." In this throw-away irony about her body weight, Huxley makes her shallowness plainer than ever.

But she still wants to go with Bernard to America to see the Savage Reservation, something that few people are allowed to do.

In the second scene, Bernard goes to get his permit for the trip initialed. The Director stops acting like a caricature of a bureaucrat and tells Bernard how he had gone to the same Reservation as a young man, 25 years before. Bernard, for all his desire to be different, is disturbed because the Director *is* being different: he is talking about something that happened a long time ago, which is very bad manners in this society.

The Director is obviously remembering events that affected him very deeply. The girlfriend he had taken to the Reservation wandered off and got lost while he was asleep. Search parties never found her, and the Director assumed she had died in some kind of accident. He still dreams about it, which means that even he has more individual feelings than the system thinks is good for you.

The Director suddenly realizes that he has revealed more about himself than is good for his reputation. He stops reminiscing and attacks Bernard, who has been unlucky enough to be his unintended audience. He scolds Bernard for *not* being infantile in his emotional life, and threatens him with transfer to Iceland as a punishment.

His status as a rebel makes Bernard feel pleased with himself. But when he goes to see Helmholtz, he doesn't get the praise he expects. Helmholtz doesn't like the way Bernard switches back and forth from boasting to self-pity, the way he knows what to do only after he should have done it, when it's too late.

The third scene takes Bernard and Lenina across the ocean to Santa Fe and into the Reservation, which resembles a real-world Navajo or Hopi reservation. The Warden of the Reservation is a replica of the cartoon-like Director, pumping an endless flow of unwanted information. Bernard remembers that he left the Eau de Cologne tap in his bathroom open, pumping an expensive flow of unwanted scent. He calls Helmholtz long distance to ask him to go up and turn it off, and Helmholtz tells him that the Director has announced that he is indeed transferring Bernard to Iceland. Despite Bernard's distrust of *soma*, he takes four tablets to survive the plane trip into the Reservation. Huxley is setting the stage for the coming confrontation.

CHAPTER SEVEN

From the moment they set foot on the Reservation, Bernard and Lenina are confronted with the differences between it and their familiar world. Huxley shows the comfortable mindlessness of his Utopia by contrasting it to the startling, often ugly reality of primitive life.

This life clearly lacks the new world's stability, friendliness, and cleanliness. The Indian guide is hostile, and he smells. The Reservation is dirty, full of rubbish, dust, dogs, and flies. An old man shows what aging does to the human body when it isn't protected by conditioning and chemicals; he is toothless, wrinkled, thin, bent.

Lenina has left her *soma* in the rest-house, so she is deprived of even that form of escape. She discovers that the Indians do have some kind of community; at first, a dance reassures her by reminding her of a solidarity service and orgy-porgy. The reassurance ends when she sees people dancing with snakes, effigies of an eagle and a man nailed to a cross, and a man whipping a boy until the blood runs. She can't understand the sense of community that runs through that kind of religion.

They then confront a man who will become the greatest threat to their world's stability. He steps into their rest-house and they see that, though raised an Indian, he has blond hair and white skin, and they hear that he speaks "faultless but peculiar English."

Bernard starts questioning the Savage and soon realizes that he is the son of the Director and the woman whom the Director had brought to the Reservation from what the stranger calls the "Other Place," the Utopia. The woman had not died. She had arrived pregnant with the Director's child by an accident, a defect in a Malthusian belt. During her visit she had fallen and hurt her head, but she survived to give birth, and she had reached middle age. Her son had grown up in the pueblo. Huxley tells you that the story excites Bernard.

The young man takes them to the little house where he lives with his mother, Linda. Lenina can barely stand to look at her, fat, sick, and stinking of alcohol. But the sight of Lenina brings out Linda's memories of the Other Place that is Huxley's new world, and of all the things she learned from her conditioning. She pours out what she remembers in a confused burst of woe.

NOTE: Linda's speech helps complete the portrait of the society Huxley wants you to compare to the brave new world. Linda reveals her shame at having given birth. She complains about the shortcomings of *mescal,* the drink the Indians make (in real life as in the novel) from the mescal plant, compared to *soma,* and about the Indians' filth, their compulsion to mend clothes instead of discarding them when they get worn, and worst of all, their monogamy. The Indian women have attacked her for what she had thought of as the virtue of being promiscuous. They were asserting their own values and showing that their ideas of community, identity, and stability were the opposite of the world controllers'. Huxley doesn't romanticize these values or ideas, though. The Savage Reservation may not suffer under the sophisticated oppression of London, but neither is it paradise.

CHAPTER EIGHT

In this chapter John, Linda's son, the young Savage, tells Bernard the story of his life. Huxley gives you broad hints that John will have a unique perspective on the brave new world because he inherited the genes and some of the culture of Utopia while growing up in the primitive culture of the Reservation.

As a boy, John witnessed his mother's painful shift from the happy sex life of Utopia to being the victim of both the Indian men who came to her bed and the Indian women who punished her for violating their laws. As her son, he, too, was an outsider—barred from marrying the Indian girl he loved and from being initiated into the tribe. He was denied the tribe's community and identity.

Instead, he went through the Indian initiation rituals of fasting and dreaming on his own, and learned something about suffering. He discovered time, death, and God—things about which the citizens of Utopia have only very limited knowledge. He discovered them not in the company of other boys his age, but *alone*. When Bernard hears this, he says he feels the same way because he's different. Huxley wants you to compare John's aloneness with Bernard's. Which do you think is more complete, more painful? Is it possible to be truly alone in the civilization of the Other Place?

John used Linda's stories of the Other Place as the first building blocks of his own mental world. He added the Indian stories he heard. And he crowned the mixture with what he found in a copy of Shakespeare that somehow made its way onto the Reservation. The book educated him in reading and in the English language. Shakespeare means no more to Bernard and Lenina than to the Indians, because he is part of the dust of history that the Controller whisked away in Chapter 3. But John finds a reference in Shakespeare for everything he feels.

NOTE: Here we see where Huxley found the title for his book. When Bernard comes up with a scheme to take John and Linda back to London, John loves the idea. He quotes lines from *The Tempest* that Huxley expects the reader to know even if Bernard doesn't. They are spoken by Miranda, the innocent daughter of Prospero, a deposed duke and functioning magician. She has grown up on a desert island where she has known only two spirits and one human being, her father. She falls in love with a handsome young nobleman who has been shipwrecked on their island, and then meets his equally gracious father and friends, and she says: "O, wonder! How many goodly creatures are there here! How beauteous mankind is! O brave new world, that has such people in it."

John doesn't intend to be ironic when he uses the lines as he contemplates plunging into his new world, but Huxley does. Bernard enables you to see the irony, and Huxley's true feelings about his bad Utopia, when he says to John, "Hadn't you better wait till you actually see the new world?"

CHAPTER NINE

This short chapter sets up the steps from confrontation to climax, the decisive point in the development of the story. Lenina goes on an 18-hour *soma* "trip" to escape from the horrors she encountered on the Reservation. Bernard helicopters to Sante Fe and puts in a long-distance call to Mustapha Mond, the Controller, back in London. He tells Mond the story of Linda and John—and presumably of the Director. Huxley doesn't spell that out, but you know it's true because you know that Bernard wants to protect himself from the Director's threat of exile in Iceland, and because Huxley told you in Chapter Eight that Bernard had been "secretly elaborating" a strategy from the moment he realized who John's father must be. Mond issues orders to bring them back to London.

Indeed Bernard is plotting his own advancement, as you can see from the way he shows off to the Warden about the orders to take John and Linda back with him. He likes to think he's different from his fellows, but he also wants to be accepted or, better, looked up to. Yet he *is* being different; most of the citizens of the brave new world wouldn't dare to do what he's now doing. In this world, being different may threaten community, identity, and stability. Do you think Bernard's actions threaten those goals? Do you think he intends to make such threats? He might endanger them without wanting to.

Meanwhile John observes Lenina asleep. He has fallen in love with her as quickly as Miranda with Ferdinand, or Romeo with Juliet, and he quotes *Romeo and Juliet* to her as she sleeps. This sublime emotion marks him as a Savage, in contrast to the civilized worldlings who believe in their commandment to be promiscuous: "Everyone belongs to everyone else." John believes instead in an idea he found among the Indians but knows better in Shakespearean language, the idea of "pure and vestal modesty." ("Vestal" is the name of ancient Roman priestesses who had to be virgins.) He does have sexual feelings: he thinks of unzipping Lenina and then hates himself for the mere thought. Do you think she would understand this if she woke up and heard him murmuring to himself?

John is aroused from his reverie by the return of Bernard's rather un-Shakespearean helicopter. Huxley had not yet written any film scripts when he wrote this book, but he is using a screenwriting technique, making the helicopter prepare you visually for a change of scene in the next chapter. Perhaps his poor vision made him more conscious of the need to see things happen, and to make the reader see things happen.

CHAPTER TEN

The scene indeed shifts abruptly—back to the London Hatchery and Conditioning Centre. The novel's first climax is about to occur: John and Linda's plunge into the brave new Utopia, the thrusting of unorthodox, emotional humans into the world of orthodox, emotionless clones.

The Director, as the chapter opens, is working to maintain orthodoxy. He is going to make a public announcement of Bernard's transfer to Iceland as punishment for the "scandalous unorthodoxy" of his sex life, his refusal to behave like a baby and seek instant gratification. As far as the Director is concerned, Bernard's emotional sins are all the greater because of his intellectual eminence.

The Director doesn't know he is about to be confronted with a much greater unorthodoxy from his own past. In the presence of all the high-caste workers of the Fertilizing Room, he announces the transfer and gives Bernard what is meant to be a purely formal opportunity to make a plea for himself. Bernard replies by bringing in Linda, "a strange and terrifying monster of middle-agedness," who recognizes the Director as her lover of a generation earlier and greets him with affection.

When he responds with disgust, her face twists "grotesquely into the grimace of extreme grief," an emotion that of course is completely foreign to civilized people in this world. She screams, "You made me have a baby," which fills the Director and all the others there with real horror.

Linda calls in John, who enters, falls on his knees in front of the Director, and says, "My father!" That turns the horror into a comic obscenity. The Director is humiliated. He puts his hands over his ears to protect them from the obscene word—"father"—and rushes out of the room. The listeners, almost hysterical, upset tube after tube of spermatozoa, another example of Huxley's grimly appropriate jokes.

CHAPTER ELEVEN

All the important characteristics of the brave new world and its people are visible in this chapter, though the action does not carry the plot much further forward. After you finish reading it, decide whether you regard the chapter as a peak or a plateau, an exciting vision or a restful summary.

Everybody who is important in London wants to see John, the true Savage. Nobody wants to see Linda, who had been decanted just as they had been, who committed the obscene act of becoming a mother, and who is fat and ugly. Linda doesn't care, however, because she has come back to civilization—which for her is a *soma* holiday that lasts longer and longer—and that will kill her, though she doesn't know it. Is Huxley really saying that everyone in this Utopia is in the same fix, but doesn't know it?

As John's guardian, Bernard Marx is suddenly popular and successful with women. Huxley shows you how hollow Bernard's success is in two ways: he lets you see that Bernard's friend Helmholtz is not impressed but only saddened because Bernard has revealed that he really is like everybody else; and he tells you that people still don't really like Bernard or the way he criticizes the established order.

Bernard takes the Savage to see all the high points of the World State, a literary trick from older, classical Utopias that enables Huxley to satirize both the real world and the brave new world. One of the simplest examples is the official who brags that a rocket travels 1,250 kilometers an hour—not unlike an airline ad in one of today's newspapers. John responds by remembering that Ariel, the good spirit of Shakespeare's *Tempest,* could travel around the world in 40 minutes.

Bernard and John also visit a coeducational Eton, where Bernard makes advances toward the Head Mistress. This is another joke that Huxley aims at his English readers. He attended Eton, probably the most elite school in England—then and now a school for boys only.

Huxley really wants you to notice the Eton students laughing at a movie showing Savages in pain as they whip themselves for their sins, and that with the help of toys and chocolate creams, the students are conditioned to lose any fear of death. The Head Mistress says death is "like any other physiological process." Huxley follows her comment by saying that she and Bernard have a date for eight that night at the Savoy. He does not have to actually say that they plan to experience a different physiological process. This is an example of Huxley's wit and elegance, the ability to say much in few words.

The satire on both real and Utopian worlds continues when the scene switches to Lenina and Fanny. Thanks to her new-found fame, Lenina has slept with many very important people, like the Ford Chief Justice (in England, the chief justice is a lord) and the Arch-Community Songster of Canterbury (the Archbishop of Canterbury is the chief clergyman in the Church of England). They all ask her what it's like to make love to a Savage, but she still doesn't know; John has maintained his purity against Utopia's promiscuity.

The highlight of this scene is the song that says, "Love's as good as *soma*." This is an important variation on a theme; the people of *Brave New World* use their promiscuity to escape dull routine, just the way they use the drug.

John's purity even survives a trip to the feelies with Lenina. Because she knows the celebrity Savage, Lenina has already been on the Feelytone news. Huxley mentions television as a feature of the brave new world, anticipating something that became available to the public over 15 years after he wrote this book. However, he didn't anticipate that television news programs would end movie newsreels. "Feelytone" is a parody on Movietone News, one of the leading newsreels of the 1930s.

The feely shows a black making love to a blonde, which reminds John of Shakespeare's *Othello*. Huxley reminds you in this chapter, as he does throughout the book, that the Utopian caste system resembles real-world racial discrimination, though he takes pains to show that Deltas and Epsilons, at the bottom of the pecking order, may be white *or* black.

John's feelings about the feelies are not happy. He thinks the erotic touch of the show is "ignoble," and he thinks he's noble for not making love to Lenina as she expects and wants him to.

CHAPTER TWELVE

The characters and their ideas come into conflict again in this chapter. First Bernard invites important guests to meet the Savage, but John refuses to leave his room. The guests immediately start to feel contempt for Bernard, whom they had pretended to like only to meet John. Bernard again becomes a victim of the system, and again suffers the feeling of being different that plagued him before.

John likes Bernard better that way, and so does Helmholtz, who has become John's friend. Helmholtz recites verses he wrote about solitude, a sin against the Utopian system; John responds with some of Shakespeare's verses on the self. Helmholtz is entranced, and is annoyed when Bernard equates a Shakespearean metaphor with orgy-porgy. But Helmholtz himself is a creature of Utopia. He thinks it absurdly comical that Juliet has a mother and that she wants to give herself to one man but not to another. He says a poet in the modern world must find some other pain, some other madness to write well. Actually, he says a "propaganda technician" must find these feelings, seeing no difference between that label and "poet." The chapter ends with his wondering what madness and violence he can find—a signal that Huxley wants you to wonder, too, and to suspect that the answer will soon become plain.

CHAPTER THIRTEEN

In this chapter the conflict between John and Lenina reaches its peak.

Lenina, distraught over John's failure to make love to her, goes to his apartment determined to make love to him. At first he is delighted to see her and tells her she means so much to him that he wanted to do something to show he was worthy of her. He wants to marry her. She can't understand either the Shakespearean or the ordinary words he uses because the idea of a lifelong, exclusive relationship is completely foreign to her. If she did understand it, it would be either a horror or an obscene joke, like Linda's motherhood.

She does finally understand, however, that John loves her. Her reaction is immediate: she strips off her clothes and presses up against him, ready for the enthusiastic sex that is as close as this system comes to love. John becomes furious, calls her a whore, and tells her to get out of his sight; when she goes into the bathroom, he begins to recite Shakespearean lines that say that sex is vulgar.

What do you think about this scene? Huxley has made plain throughout the book that he doesn't like the promiscuity of the brave new world. But is he taking John's side here? At one moment he seems to, but at others he suggests that John's attitude is madness, and he certainly brings John close to violence.

CHAPTER FOURTEEN

The book moves from sex and love in Chapter 13 to love and death in this chapter. John rushes to the Park Lane Hospital for the Dying, where his mother, Linda, has been taken. All the *soma* she has been using has put her into a state of "imbecile happiness." Those words seldom appear together; joining them creates a phrase of immense strength that tells us Huxleys' real attitude toward his Utopia. Seeing her makes John remember the Utopia she described to him when he was a child, the brave new world in his head that contrasts so painfully with the Utopia he now lives in.

A group of Delta children comes in for their weekly conditioning in seeing death as a natural process, and John is furious at their invasion of his grief. He is also furious when, in her delirium, his mother fails to recognize him and thinks he is Popé, her chief lover from the Reservation. Linda dies, and John collapses in tears. This threatens to destroy the conditioning the Deltas are receiving, and the nurse in charge has to give them chocolate éclairs to remind them that death is a natural and happy event.

NOTE: Huxley wants to show how monstrous it is to deny the emotions of grief and loss. He hates a process that conditions people not to feel those emotions, that sorrow can be erased with gooey pastry. He doesn't mention any way of learning to experience mourning without being destroyed by it, though. Perhaps he is reflecting here his grief over the death of his own mother when he was only 14.

CHAPTER FIFTEEN

John leaves Linda's deathbed and plunges into the midst of the daily distribution of *soma* to the Deltas who work in the hospital. He thinks again of Miranda's words—but mockingly this time—as he looks at the Deltas, and says, over and over again, "O brave new world." He feels a challenge in the words, a challenge to turn the nightmare into something noble, so he tries to stop the distribution of the *soma,* telling the Deltas that their precious drug is poison and imagining that he can urge them to freedom. John is still the Savage, and he has the savage idea that any person can be free; apparently he still can't imagine the real nature of conditioning.

Bernard and Helmholtz learn that John is going mad at the Hospital for the Dying. They rush to meet him and find they have to save him from the mob of Deltas, maddened and frustrated because he has thrown away their *soma.* The police restore order; although this new world is one in which everyone is happy and hardly anyone breaks the law, the police still come when they're needed. Like Bernard's suspicion of spies at the door in Chapter 4, this scene anticipates Orwell's *1984,* though with a much gentler police state. Helmholtz, Bernard, and John are arrested. In every stage of this scene, Bernard seems to be trying to escape the consequences of the difference between himself and other Utopians that in other moments he is proud of.

CHAPTER SIXTEEN

This chapter begins the final climax of *Brave New World,* which continues into Chapter 17. The friends who can't accept the system confront the man who speaks for the system—the Controller, Mustapha Mond. As usual, John and Helmholtz speak their minds, and so does the Controller; as usual, only Bernard worries about the "unpleasant realities of the situation."

The Controller knows Shakespeare, it turns out—knowledge forbidden to the ordinary elite. He who makes the laws is free to break the laws, he says. Huxley wants to remind you that many real-life rulers have taken the same attitude.

The Controller explains that Shakespeare is forbidden both because it's old and beautiful, qualities that might make people turn against the synthetic beauty of the brave new world, and because the people wouldn't understand it. In the new world, there can be no great art because it's impossible to have both happiness and high art at the same time; "you can't make tragedies without social instability." This returns the scene (and you) to the basic theme of the book, the need for stability.

The Controller acknowledges that stability has none of the glamour or picturesque quality of a fight against misfortune or a struggle against temptation. He says happiness and contentment are worth the loss. Do you think Huxley agrees? Or is he saying that that fight, that struggle, is necessary for a truly good life? The chapter doesn't tell you what he thinks; you have to decide the issue for yourself.

The Controller also explains why society cannot function with nothing but Alphas—they won't do the dirty work, the work Epsilons *like* doing. The Controllers once tried to create an experimental society composed only of Alphas, and it led to a civil war that killed 19,000 of the 22,000 discontented Alphas. The lower castes, he says, find happiness in their work, happiness that guarantees stability.

NOTE: Here you see that the brave new world has stifled not only art and religion but also the science that first gave it the tools of control and that it still pretends to worship. Keeping the populace stable prevents this society from using most of its scientific knowledge. If it did use this knowledge, science would produce inventions that would reduce the need for Delta and Epsilon labor; the lower castes would then become unhappy and threaten stability. Mustapha Mond knows the tragedy of this better than anyone else, because he was a first-class scientist who gave up science to be a ruler—a ruler of a society that constantly invokes the name of science. Huxley was making fun of English and American society; in 1931, he couldn't have known how well he was describing the future development of Nazi Germany and Soviet Russia, which pretended to worship science but actually crippled it.

The Controller has to deal with the three friends, who in his terms are dissidents, like the people in the Soviet Union whom the newspapers call dissidents—people who can't accept the wrongs they see in their society. He sends Bernard to Iceland and Helmholtz to the Falkland Islands. Bernard objects, pathetically; Helmholtz doesn't, because he accepts the Controller's notion that a small island, distant from the metropolis, is the right place for people who are too individual to fit into community life in this Utopia. England is an island, of course, but it's clearly too large, too central, and too highly populated to be a good place for unorthodox individuals. Huxley's love of and fantasy about islands, signaled here, later inspired his novel of a good Utopia, *Island*.

CHAPTER SEVENTEEN

After determining the fate of Bernard and Helmholtz, the Controller still has to deal with John, the Savage, in the climactic confrontation of the book. John insists the world has paid a high price for happiness by giving up art and science. The Controller adds religion to this list and quotes at length from two 19th-century religious figures in order to conclude that "God isn't compatible with machinery and scientific medicine and universal happiness."

NOTE: This is one of the fundamental principles of the brave new world, though only the controller knows that. Do you think it's true? Does Huxley think it's true? You should be able to figure out that he doesn't—by listening carefully for the tones of voice in which John and Mond speak, especially in their exchange of ideas about God.

John sees it as natural for people to believe in God when they are most alone. Mond says they have made it almost impossible to be alone. John knows he suffered equally from being shut out of the Indian community and from being unable to escape the civilized community. Do you feel that just by mentioning those two opposites, Huxley suggests a third, a compromise, is possible?

John also sees God as one who manages, punishes, and rewards. Huxley never says he agrees with John, and often he doesn't, but he keeps using the Savage to point up the hollow quality of the Controller's ideas, again using classic Utopian devices.

This is clear when Mond says that Edmund, one of the villains in Shakespeare's *King Lear*, would not be punished in the new world, only thrust into its "pleasant vices," and John says that that itself would be a punishment for Edmund. It becomes even clearer when the Controller tells John that passion means instability and instability means the end of civilization, that a properly organized society has no need of the noble or heroic. Huxley is telling you here as plainly as he can that this is a bad Utopia.

But the Controller knows that passion is part of the definition of humanity; even in the brave new world people take monthly treatments of Violent Passion Surrogate, which floods their bodies with the same hormone that would flow through them if they felt real fear and rage. The Savage rejects this idea and claims the right to be unhappy, the right to suffer illness, pain, and fear. The Controller tells John he can have them. In one sense, Mond understands why John wants them; in another, he can't really understand that anyone would make that choice. You can read both reactions in the shrug of the shoulders that ends the chapter.

CHAPTER EIGHTEEN

John opens this chapter by making himself throw up—a crude but brilliant metaphor for his claim to the right to be unhappy, and for his need to purify himself after "eating" civilization and what he sees as his own wickedness.

He tells Bernard and Helmholtz that he, too, asked to be sent to an island, and that the Controller refused because he wanted "to go on with the experiment." The Controller apparently didn't realize that John was capable of refusing to go on with it.

Instead, the Savage sets himself up as a hermit in an abandoned air-lighthouse once used to show helicopters their proper air route. He is discovered by accident while whipping himself in a penitential rite. Reporters soon descend on him and make a news story out of everything, even the kick he delivers to one reporter's coccyx. (Huxley wrote in a world and time when a civilized writer didn't put certain phrases in print.)

One of the things John punishes himself for is his sexual desire for Lenina. Huxley shows you that even an idealist can feel lust; John is learning the truth that the Controller recognized in the previous chapter, that passion is part of the definition of humanity.

A mob of tourists descends, much worse than the reporters. Worst of all, one of them is Lenina. Like fans at a boxing match or hockey game, they become crazed with fear and fascination when John starts to whip Lenina as well as himself. He chants "Kill it, kill it" (meaning "kill fleshy desire"), as Lenina writhes at his feet. An orgy of beating possesses the mob and becomes an orgy-porgy. When John wakes up the next morning, he hates himself with new intensity. Huxley never says that he actually has sex with Lenina or that he kills her, but it's not important; the thought that he might have done either one is enough to make John want to kill himself. When a new crowd arrives that evening, they find he has.

Why do you think John chooses death? Did he have to choose between death and the stable, mindless happiness of the brave new world? In the Foreword, Huxley says he gave John only two alternatives: what he saw as an insane life for the Savage in Utopia, and what he called the lunacy of a primitive life in an Indian village, "more human in some respects, but in others hardly less queer or abnormal." At the end of the novel, John could not tolerate either alternative and found a third choice: suicide.

In the 1946 Foreword, Huxley said he could see a third choice that would have made suicide unnecessary, a choice he hadn't seen when he first wrote the book—a compromise in which science would serve man, economics would be decentralized, and politics cooperative rather than coercive. Much later he wrote *Island*, a novel about a good Utopia, in which he developed some of those ideas.

A STEP BEYOND

Tests and Answers

TESTS

Test 1

1. The exposition of this novel is accomplished through the use of ____B____
   A. a separate introductory essay
   B. a tour for new students through the Central London Hatchery
   C. a question-and-answer dialogue between the Director and his new assistant

2. Children are taught morals in their sleep through a process called ____A____
   A. hypnopaedia
   B. decanting
   C. consumerism

3. For their holiday, Bernard and Lenina go to ____C____
   A. the moon
   B. London
   C. New Mexico

4. Bernard's idiosyncrasies are generally explained by ____B____
   A. a poor family life
   B. alcohol in his blood surrogate
   C. his infatuation with Lenina

5. The Solidarity Service which everyone must attend usually ends ____A____
   A. in an orgy
   B. with a deep religious revelation
   C. when the clocks strike thirteen

6. People are taught to hate nature because C
   - A. there are not enough trees left
   - B. they would be allergic to natural substances
   - C. it doesn't cost anything to enjoy nature

7. Each person's social rank is predetermined in order to C
   - A. insure an adequate number of workers for each function
   - B. create a stable society
   - C. both A and B

8. Ford occupies a position of reverence because A
   - A. he invented the assembly line
   - B. everyone has a car
   - C. both A and B

9. *Soma* is B
   - A. the day of rest
   - B. a drug
   - C. the major religion of this future world

10. A motto of this new world is C
    - A. Sex and Soma
    - B. Alpha, Beta, Gamma, Delta, Epsilon
    - C. Community, Identity, Stability

11. *Brave New World* is a novel of ideas. Discuss what this does to the characters and the plot, giving three examples of different ways that Huxley presents ideas.

12. *Brave New World* is a Utopia. Describe the goals of its ideal state and the state's general principles for achieving them, and give three examples of particular techniques that illustrate those principles.

13. How does *Brave New World* satirize the present day? Describe three particular vices and follies that are its targets.

14. *Brave New World* keeps asking how much it would cost to achieve the benefits of the new society. What are the benefits? Does Huxley think the price is high or low? Do you agree? Discuss in terms of three specific costs.

15. Discuss Huxley's attitude toward science. Does he think the brave new world uses it well? Does he think it's possible to use it well?

Test 2

1. The Indians made Linda an outcast because ______
- A. they considered her an immoral woman
- B. she was white
- C. she considered herself better than the Indians

2. Bernard brings Linda and John back to London because ______
- A. he thinks this will be an interesting experiment in cross-cultural studies
- B. he wants to embarrass the Director
- C. he is falling in love with Linda

3. John learned to read by reading the work of ______
- A. Ford
- B. Freud
- C. Shakespeare

4. "If one's different one's bound to be lonely. They're beastly to one. Do you know, they shut me out of absolutely everything?" This was said by ______
- A. Bernard
- B. Helmholtz
- C. John

5. As John's guardian, Bernard finds that he is suddenly ______
- A. jealous

B. too busy to do his job
C. popular

6. John falls in love with ___A___
A. Lenina
B. a Delta minus
C. the Director's wife

7. When Linda dies, John ___C___
A. is glad she's gone to a final rest
B. decides to return to the Reservation
C. starts a riot at the Hospital for the Dying

8. In his discussion with Mustapha Mond, John claims ___B___
A. he is willing to adapt to the customs of the new world
B. the right to be unhappy
C. he never really belonged on the Reservation

9. Bernard and Helmholtz are to be ___C___
A. executed
B. reprogrammed
C. sent to an island

10. John's final answer to the "brave new world" is to ___C___
A. start an underground anarchist group
B. go back to the Reservation
C. commit suicide

11. Analyze the personality of Bernard Marx, giving three examples of his thoughts, feelings, and actions at critical moments.

12. Discuss Lenina as a person, as a citizen, as a woman. What are her functions in this novel?

13. Discuss three ways that John the Savage differs from the citizens of the Other Place. What do his thoughts and feelings enable you to see about the Utopia?

14. Discuss *Brave New World* as a look at the future, analyzing the difference between prophecy and prediction.

15. Discuss sex, sports, and *soma*. What do they have in common and how do they differ from the point of view of the individual citizen and of the state?

ANSWERS

Test 1

1. B **2.** A **3.** C **4.** B **5.** A **6.** C

7. C **8.** A **9.** B **10.** C

11. Every section of this guide can help you answer this question. Some characters exist only to express or embody a particular idea, and some have something close to three-dimensional, live personalities. Huxley expresses some ideas by putting them in the mouths of cartoon characters like the Director; some by making them part of serious dialogue, like the conversations between Bernard and Helmholtz and between the Controller and John; and some by actual behavior, like Lenina's sex life with Henry Foster and Bernard, and her attempt with John.

Compare the different kinds of characters and say what you like and don't like about them. How do their ideas affect their actions and their personalities, and vice versa?

Look for specific chapters where the plot stands still while ideas are expressed, and compare the "action" to a chapter in which the characters really do things and relate to each other. Which category does Chapter 17, in which the Controller and the Savage argue, belong in?

12. The goals of the world state are mentioned in the first paragraph of the book and frequently thereafter, and they are mentioned also in this guide. They are community, identity, and stability. The general principle for achieving them is to use new scientific techniques to make people like to do what they *have* to do, as the Director says in Chapter 1, and to eliminate every painful emotion, as the Controller says in Chapter 3 and Chapter 17. Among the many specific techniques embodying those principles are the different kinds of conditioning; the use of *soma*, sex, and sports; the training about death; the elimination of history and literature. You should focus on three in detail.

13. This kind of satire is a matter of exaggerating behavior that Huxley saw around him and projecting it into the future. Look for vices and follies in the use of science, religion, the economic structure, and the attitude toward sex, in every theme and every chapter. Almost everything that the book satirizes existed either in the 1920s or today, but you may have to think about some or do research on others, like particular church practices. It would also be interesting to decide which is a vice and which a folly.

14. The benefits are the achievement of community, identity, and stability, if you prize them as the Controllers do, and the absence of war, poverty, disease, and social unrest. What do you think about them as benefits? What price would you be willing to pay for them?

Huxley thinks the cost in *Brave New World* is far too high. You can find some costs mentioned in the first three chapters and others in Chapters 16 and 17; they are summarized under Theme 11 in this guide. You can write an A (or alpha) paper if you think carefully about the value that *you* put on the benefits and the costs.

15. Huxley says in his 1946 Foreword that the theme of *Brave New World* is "the advancement of science as it affects human individuals." He had some scientific training before he lost his vision, and believed that scientific advances could and would be made, but he didn't trust scientists or rulers to use them properly. He foresaw danger in most scientific and technological discoveries—the danger that their use would turn into abuse and produce evil. The whole point of *Brave New World* is that it does not use science well. But as the guide tells you, Huxley never gave up on the possibility of using science well, and made that possibility a reality in his last novel, *Island*.

Test 2

1. A	**2.** B	**3.** C	**4.** C	**5.** C	**6.** A
7. C	**8.** B	**9.** C	**10.** C		

11. Bernard feels different because of his small size, and that sense of difference enables him to see what is wrong in the brave new world and to imagine alternatives. But he lacks courage and secretly wants to succeed on the society's own terms. You should have no trouble finding examples of either criticisms or failures in his first appearance, his trip to the Reservation, his relations with John and Helmholtz, his involvement with Lenina, or his distress at being exiled. You can write a better answer if you compare him to Helmholtz, who is different in another way.

12. Lenina is an exemplary citizen except for one peculiarity that makes her more of an individual than most citizens: she will sometimes date or sleep with only one man at a time for as long as four months, violating the commandment to be promiscuous. As a female, she is particularly "pneumatic"—usually taken to mean that she has attractive breasts, but perhaps also meaning that she is especially exciting during intercourse. As a woman, her main function is to excite feelings in Bernard and John that show their respective differences from brave new worldlings. A feminist might say it is ironic that although she has little personality of her own, she takes the sexual initiative with John, something that many people think only a strong woman can do. Huxley implies that this is not uncommon in the brave new world, though it seldom happened in real life in his own day.

13. John is different in many ways, starting with his birth: he was born from a woman, not decanted from a bottle. He grew up an outsider among the Savages instead of a member of a defined group. He grew up without conditioning, but with a knowledge of Shakespeare and of the Savages' religion. He grew up loving and hating his mother. He knows the value of suffering and pain.

Many Utopias contrast civilized and "savage" behavior. John has the full range of emotions that citizens of the new world lack, and this enables him and you to see how hollow some of the virtues of the Utopia are. If you look at several feelings in particular, you will find that each one provides a new perspective on a different aspect of Utopia. John's feelings about his mother's death, for instance, give you a dramatic insight into the new world's conditioning about death.

14. Look up the dictionary definitions of "prophecy" and "prediction"; then look at what Huxley says in his Foreword. The novel is an inaccurate prediction of specific facts; it never mentions atomic energy, for instance. But 15 years after he wrote it, Huxley thought it was a good warning of the dangers of certain developments in biology and psychology, a good prophecy of changes in sexual morality.

15. They all offer escape from the routine of everyday life, and their use is encouraged by the state to keep citizens happy. Individuals play or watch sports more compulsively than we do because they've been conditioned to like them, but they don't get as much pleasure from sports as they do from sex, and not quite as complete an escape in sex as they do in *soma*. Sex still requires two people, while *soma* is a solitary experience in a world that offers few of these. The state seems to regard all three as necessary but to give *soma* the highest priority, with sex second and sports third. Look for quotations about each experience. At one point, Lenina sings, "Love's as good as *soma*." Do you think this is literally true from the worldlings' point of view?

Term Paper Ideas

Utopias

1. Compare *Brave New World,* Huxley's bad Utopia, with *Island,* his good one.

2. How does the society prophesied by *Brave New World* compare with today's reality?

3. Why do the creators of Utopias introduce savages into their new worlds? (Hint: looking at ideal states through the eyes of a primitive stranger provides deeper and more colorful visions.)

Community, Identity, Stability

1–3. How is each one achieved in the brave new world? (Hint: see the section of this guide on themes.)

Science

1. What scientific developments did *Brave New World* foresee? How much of its scientific prophecy has come true?

2. Why did Huxley emphasize chemical and psychological conditioning rather than make super weapons or nuclear energy elements of his new world? (Hint: he was interested in science that could affect man without killing him, and his Utopia took other advances for granted.)

3. How does the controlled breeding of *Brave New World* compare to the recent changes in genetic engineering in the real world?

Conditioning

1. Why does the Utopia use chemical and physical conditioning on embryos in bottles? (Look at the specific conditioning achieved.)

2. Why does the Utopia use hypnopaedia to condition babies? (Distinguish between teaching facts and teaching moral attitudes while you sleep.)

3. In what ways are we "conditioned" today? By what? Whom? From what motivations? For what purposes?

Sexual Pleasure

1. Why does the Utopia encourage people to be promiscuous?

2. Would I like to live in a world where everyone belongs to everyone else? (Analyze why and why not.)

3. Would Malthusian drill be something we could borrow from *Brave New World* to deal with teenage pregnancy? (Again, why and why not?)

Soma

1. Why is this drug a supreme necessity in the brave new world? (Hint: keep people happy by enabling them to escape.) Why is this a perversion of Huxley's hopes for a perfect drug? (Hint: it doesn't help you achieve knowledge of God; see section on Themes in this guide.)

2. How does the Utopia's use of *soma* compare with real-world use of alcohol, tobacco, marijuana, and cocaine?

3. In what ways can and are drugs used in a positive way today? In a negative way? What dangers does Huxley want us to avoid?

Other Pleasures

1. How would I feel about the Feelies?

2. How would I feel about *Brave New World* sports? (Include your thoughts about Huxley's failure to give details and on his using the names as a joke.)

Religion

1. In what way is "Ford" in *Brave New World* like "Christ" in our world? In what ways are the two different?

2. Why do you think Huxley chose to mythologize Ford (and briefly Freud) in *Brave New World?*

Family

1. Why does the Utopia make family an obscene joke or a crime? (Hint: Huxley says it's because families produce neuroses. Could it also be that the family is a focus of loyalty that might compete with the state?)

2. Compare the idea of family in *Brave New World* with a Utopia you create that redesigns a family to make people happy. (What changes would you make in your own family?)

Death

1. Death as a natural process—how the Utopia sees it, and how I see it.

2. Why the brave new world tries to eliminate the sense of loss and grief.

The Costs of Utopia

1. What are the costs of achieving the good aspects of the brave new world? (Describe the benefits of the world and their costs—including costs like the loss of family and the loss of art. Estimate whether the costs are high or low, and compare your estimate to Huxley's.)

Further Reading

AUTHOR'S OTHER WORKS

Many of Huxley's other books are worth reading. Listed here are those that provide particular additional insights into *Brave New World.*

Crome Yellow, 1921.

Point Counter-Point, 1928. Like *Crome Yellow,* this book gives you an earlier view of some of the ideas developed in *Brave New World* and provides characters to compare with those of the Utopian novel.

The Perennial Philosophy, 1945.

The Doors of Perception, 1954. In this book and in *The Perennial Philosophy,* Huxley explores the ideas of mystic communion and drugs.

Brave New World Revisited, 1958. Huxley treats in essay form many of the same topics he explored 25 years earlier in his novel: overpopulation, overorganization, propaganda, and chemical conditioning, among other subjects. "The nightmare of total organization . . . has emerged from the safe, remote future and is now awaiting us, just around the next corner." The book ends with two chapters on what people can do to prevent the nightmare from becoming reality. Huxley wanted to lower the world birth rate, increase food production, renew the environment, and decentralize political and economic power. He also wanted to create a system of education that would make propaganda and conditioning more difficult to abuse.

Island, 1962. This novel about a good Utopia shows that Huxley never gave up his belief in the benefits of science or of a drug that would enable man to transcend the limits of the self and know God, despite the warnings he gave against the misuse of science and drugs in *Brave New World.* The people of Pala, a fictional island in the Indian Ocean, enjoy a stable population, healthy agriculture, marvelous preventive medicine, no heavy industry, and an economy that is neither capitalist nor socialist. They also use *moksha*-medicine, a perfected version of LSD, to have religious visions that enable them to achieve a union with God. And, as in *Brave New World*, they use chemicals to condition babies—but with a major difference: on Pala such techniques are employed only to eliminate aggression or to raise the intelligence of retarded children to within normal range.

OTHER WORKS ABOUT UTOPIA

Three novels by other writers can be compared to *Brave New World*.

Orwell, George. *1984* (1948). A novel of an even grimmer future than that portrayed by Huxley.

Wells, H.G. *Men Like Gods* (1923). The novel Huxley intended to satirize in his own Utopia.

Zamyatin, Yevgeny. *We* (1959). A portrayal of the future inspired by the repression within the Soviet Union, the book bears some resemblances to *Brave New World* and influenced George Orwell.

CRITICAL WORKS

Bedford, Sybille. *Aldous Huxley: A Biography*. New York: Alfred A. Knopf, 1974. Essential to understand how Huxley's life related to his writings.

Bowering, Peter. *Aldous Huxley: A Study of the Major Novels*. New York: Oxford University Press, 1969. One of the more useful critical studies.

Brander, Laurence. *Aldous Huxley: A Critical Study*. Lewisburg, Pa.: Bucknell University Press, 1970. Another useful study.

Firchow, Peter. *Aldous Huxley: Satirist and Novelist*. Minneapolis, Mn.: University of Minnesota Press, 1972. One of the more useful critical studies.

Kuehn, Robert E., editor. *Aldous Huxley: A Collection of Critical Essays*. Englewood Cliffs, N.J.: Prentice-Hall, 1974.

Meckier, Jerome. *Aldous Huxley: Satire and Structure*. London: Chatto and Windus, 1969.

Watts, Harold H. *Aldous Huxley*. New York: Twayne, 1969.

Glossary

Anthrax An infectious, often fatal disease of sheep and cattle that can also kill humans. The Utopian state was established after a war in which anthrax bombs were used as a weapon of germ warfare.

Bokanovskify; Bokanovsky's Process Method to make a human egg bud by arresting its growth, producing up to 96 identical people.

Caste One of the five groups into which all citizens of the brave new world are divided by heredity and conditioning, each with its own rank and intelligence range. They are Alpha, Beta, Gamma, Delta, and Epsilon, from the Greek letters that English schools use as grades.

Community Sing An observance of the Fordian religion for the lower castes. The Arch Community Songster is the equivalent of an Archbishop.

Condition To put into a desired state by chemical, physical, or psychological action.

Decanting Process by which embryos are removed from the bottles in which they grow; equivalent of birth.

Ectogenesis Reproduction outside the human body, for example in bottles.

Emotional Engineering Designing propaganda for use on citizens. The Utopia's closest equivalent to writing poetry.

Fitchew A Shakespearean word that John uses to curse Lenina. Literally a polecat, but in Shakespeare's day it also meant a prostitute.

Flivver An old, small, or cheap automobile. Henry Ford's original Model T was often called a flivver, so the word takes on religious meaning in the Utopia.

Freemartin A sterile person; the Utopia makes 70 percent of its females freemartins by dosing the embryos with male sex hormones. They still have female sex organs, but they also have beards that need shaving.

Gametes General term for reproductive cells of either sex.

Hypnopaedia Teaching people while they sleep. In the book, suitable only for moral suggestion, not facts or analysis.

Ova Female reproductive cells.

Podsnap's technique Method to speed the ripening of human eggs, making it possible to multiply the number a single ovary can produce.

Predestination The process of determining which embryos will grow up to do particular jobs in particular places. The word has religious overtones; it once meant God's decision as to who would be saved and who would be damned.

Pregnancy Substitute A medical technique that floods a woman's body with all the hormonal and other physical changes it would undergo during pregnancy, which she will never experience.

Savage A person who is born and raised outside the Utopia and does not know how to behave according to its rules. Savages live on Reservations surrounded by electrified fences. The Savages who appear in the book resemble Indians of the Southwest United States.

Scent Organ An instrument that plays smells the way a piano or a pipe organ plays music.

Solidarity Service A Fordian religious observance for the upper castes, usually 12 people who eventually unite in a sexual orgy.

Soma A drug that both tranquilizes and intoxicates without hangovers or side effects. It provides citizens of the Utopia with escape from self and surroundings. The word comes from the Sanskrit language of ancient India. It means both an intoxicating drink used in the old Vedic religious rituals there and the plant from whose juice the drink was made—a plant whose true identity we don't know.

Spermatozoa Male reproductive cells.

Surrogate Something selected as a substitute. Embryos grow in blood surrogate instead of real blood because they grow outside a mother's body. Morocco-surrogate is imitation leather. Violent Passion Surrogate floods the body with the same hormones that fear and rage would.

Viviparous Bearing live young rather than eggs, as mammals, including humans, do.

Zippicamiknicks Women's underwear, one-piece but sexy.

The Critics

The Price of Utopia

A life-span without war, violence and the dread of cruel disease—is it not worth the silly slogans, the scent organ, the Feelies and the lack of an unknown freedom? But the price—in our terms—is also the freedom to reject servitude, the freedom to choose, to grow, to change. The price is deep and graduated human relationships, is virtue, is courage, endurance, faith exchanged for uniformity and spiritual squalor. There is no doubt on which side Aldous comes down.

—Sybille Bedford, *Aldous Huxley: A Biography*, 1974

The Worship and Enslavement of Science

In the World-State man has been enslaved by science, or as the hypnopaedic platitude puts it, "science is everything." But, while everything owes its origin to science, science itself has been paradoxically relegated to the limbo of the past along with culture, religion, and every other worthwhile object of human endeavor. It is ironic that science, which has given the stablest equilibrium in history, should itself be regarded as a potential menace, and that all scientific progress should have been frozen since the establishment of the World-State.

—Peter Bowering, *Aldous Huxley: A Study of The Major Novels*, 1969

A Choice Between Squalor and Spiritless Happiness

The core of the book is the argument on happiness between the Controller and the Savage. They argue like a couple of Oxford dons on the name and nature of happiness in society. The Savage reveals a power in dialectic for which his past life, one would have thought, had hardly prepared him. Huxley is right. It would have been better if the Savage had had another background, something worth preferring. As it is, he has to choose between the squalor of the Reservation and the spiritless shallow happiness of the world according to Ford.

—Laurence Brander, *Aldous Huxley: A Critical Study*, 1970

America—the Brave New World?

. . . For Huxley, it is plain, there is no need to travel into the future to find the brave new world; it already exists, only too palpably, in the American Joy City, where the declaration of dependence begins and ends with the single-minded pursuit of happiness.

—Peter Firchow, *Aldous Huxley: Satirist and Novelist*, 1972